Communication Skills for your

Education

Degree

CRITICAL STUDY SKILLS

Critical Study Skills for Education Students

Our new series of study skills texts for teaching and other educational professional students has four key titles to help you succeed at your degree:

Studying for your Education Degree

Academic Writing and Referencing for your Education Degree

Critical Thinking Skills for your Education Degree

Communication Skills for your Education Degree

Register with **Critical Publishing** to:

- be the first to know about forthcoming education titles;
- find out more about our new series;
- sign up for our regular newsletter for special offers, discount codes and more.

Visit our website at:  **www.criticalpublishing.com**

Our titles are also available in a range of electronic formats. To order please go to our website www.criticalpublishing.com or contact our distributor NBN International by telephoning 01752 202301 or emailing orders@nbninternational.com.

Communication
Skills for your
Education
Degree

ANE BOTTOMLEY, KULWINDER MAUDE, STEVEN PRYJMACHUK AND DAVID WAUGH

First published in 2019 by Critical Publishing Ltd

The authors have made every effort to ensure the accuracy of information contained in this publication, but assume no responsibility for any errors, inaccuracies, inconsistencies and omissions. Likewise every effort has been made to contact copyright holders. If any copyright material has been reproduced unwittingly and without permission the Publisher will gladly receive information enabling them to rectify any error or omission in subsequent editions.

British Library Cataloguing in Publication Data
A CIP record for this book is available from the British Library

ISBN: 978-1-912508-61-7

This book is also available in the following e-book formats:
MOBI: 978-1-912508-62-4
EPUB: 978-1-912508-63-1
Adobe e-book reader: 978-1-912508-64-8

The rights of Jane Bottomley, Kulwinder Maude, Steven Pryjmachuk and David Waugh to be identified as the Authors of this work have been asserted by them in accordance with the Copyright, Design and Patents Act 1988.

Text and cover design by Out of House Limited
Project Management by Newgen Publishing UK
Printed and bound in Great Britain by 4edge, Essex

Critical Publishing
3 Connaught Road
St Albans
AL3 5RX

www.criticalpublishing.com

Paper from responsible sources

Contents

Acknowledgements

We would like to thank the many university and education students who have inspired us to write these books. Special thanks are due to Anita Gill and Patricia Cartney, and to Julia Morris at Critical Publishing for her support and editorial expertise. We are very grateful to Lindsey Vollans, Headteacher of St Michael's CE Primary, Rob Waugh, Assistant Vice Principal of the Constellation Trust and Rosemary Waugh, a recently retired teacher, for their invaluable contributions and advice.

Jane Bottomley, Kulwinder Maude, Steven Pryjmachuk and David Waugh

Meet the authors

Jane Bottomley

is a freelance writer, teacher and educational consultant. She is a Senior Fellow of the Higher Education Academy and a Senior Fellow of the BALEAP, the global forum for English for Academic Purposes practitioners. She has helped students from a wide range of disciplines to improve their academic skills and achieve their study goals, including 14 years as a Senior Language Tutor at the University of Manchester. Jane is the editor of the *Critical Study Skills* series, which covers nursing, education, social work and policing.

Kulwinder Maude

is a Senior Lecturer at Kingston University, London. She has over 20 years of experience working in different sectors of education, including extensive experience of teaching and learning in primary schools (England and India) as well as UK higher education. She teaches English on undergraduate and postgraduate Initial Teacher Education (ITE) programmes along with teaching a Masters-level module on reflective teaching. She has written articles and chapters on many aspects of primary English for ITE and primary practitioners.

Steven Pryjmachuk

is Professor of Mental Health Nursing Education in the School of Health Science's Division of Nursing, Midwifery and Social Work at the University of Manchester and a Senior Fellow of the Higher Education Academy. His teaching, clinical and research work has centred largely on supporting and facilitating individuals – be they students, patients or colleagues – to develop, learn or care independently.

David Waugh

is Professor of Education at Durham University. He has written more than 50 books on education and has taught in four schools, as well as teaching undergraduates and postgraduates and providing professional development for teachers. He has worked in universities for 29 years and still regularly teaches in schools using the children's novels he writes as a stimulus for reading, writing and discussion.

Introduction

Communication Skills for your Education Degree is the fourth book in the *Critical Study Skills for Education* series. The *Critical Study Skills for Education* series supports student teachers and other education professionals as they embark on their undergraduate degree programme. It is aimed at all student teachers, including those who have come to university straight from A levels, and those who have travelled a different route, perhaps returning to education after working and/or raising a family. The books in the series will be of use both to students from the UK, and international students who are preparing to study in a new culture – and perhaps in a second language. The books also include guidance for students with specific learning requirements.

As well as subject-specific and pedagogical knowledge and skills, teachers and other education professionals need to develop what are often described as 'soft skills', that is, communication skills and people skills. The terms 'oracy skills', 'interactional skills' and 'interpersonal skills' are also commonly used. Whichever terms are employed, the skills they describe are becoming increasingly important in university and professional settings. *Communication Skills* aims to support education students as they engage in vital oral and written communication activity in their educational studies and professional lives. It focuses on improving general oral and written communication in professional life. It also provides guidance on public speaking, in particular, academic presentations, and covers the skills you need to participate in group discussions, especially seminars. It also provides guidance on communication with lecturers during tutorials, as well as discussing the skills required for successful networking in a range of contexts, including social media. If you require more information on academic writing, related to essays or dissertations, see another book in this series, *Academic Writing and Referencing for your Education Degree*.

Between them, the authors have many years' experience of both teaching practice and education, and academic study skills. All the information, text extracts and activities in the book have a clear education focus and are often directly linked to the **Teachers' Standards**. There is also reference to relevant institutional bodies, books and journals throughout.

The many activities in the book include **tasks, reflections, top tips**, and **case studies**. There are also **advanced skills** sections, which highlight particular knowledge and skills that you will need towards the end of your degree programme – or perhaps if you go on to postgraduate study. The activities in the book often require you to work things out and discover things for yourself, a learning technique which is commonly used in universities. For many activities, there is no right or wrong answer – they might simply require you to reflect on your experience or situations you are likely to encounter at university or in your professional life; for tasks which require a particular response, there is an answer key at the back of the book.

These special features throughout the book are clearly signalled by icons to help you recognise them:

 Learning outcomes;

 Quick quiz or example exam questions / assessment tasks;

Reflection (a reflective task or activity);

 Case studies;

 Top tips;

 Checklist;

 Advanced skills information;

 Task;

 Answer provided at the back of the book.

Students with limited experience of academic life and educational practice in the UK will find it helpful to work through the book systematically; more experienced students may wish to 'dip in and out' of the book. Whichever approach you adopt, handy **cross references** signalled in the margins will help you quickly find the information that you need to focus on or revisit.

There are three **Appendices** (Academic levels at university; Key phrases in assignments; English language references) at the back of the book which you can consult as you work through the text.

We hope that this book will help you to become a successful communicator in all areas of your education studies and practice.

A note on terminology

In the context of this book, the term 'education' should be taken to include 'teaching, teacher training and the allied education professionals', wherever this is not explicitly stated.

Chapter 1
Professional speaking skills

Learning outcomes

After reading this chapter you will:

- be aware of the particular characteristics of professional, as opposed to social, communication;

- develop your understanding of the role of oral communication in the context of teaching;

- be aware of the importance of oral communication skills as a part of professional relationships;

- be aware of strategies which can help you communicate and interact with parents and carers, colleagues and third parties in a clear, appropriate and effective manner.

This chapter provides guidance to help you improve your oral communication skills in teaching and education contexts. It will present a number of strategies to help you communicate and interact with pupils and parents in a clear, appropriate and effective manner.

Communication

A human language is essentially 'a signalling system' (Barber, 2000, p 2). The signals used include sounds, written symbols such as alphabets, and signs such as those in road signals, semaphore and the sign languages used by the Deaf Community. **Communication** can be defined as the transmission or exchange of information and ideas using these signalling systems.

Communication skills are one of the core skills of teaching, and they are central to the Teachers' Standards (DfE, 2011). In this chapter, the focus is on general **oral communication**. Other chapters in this book deal with specific areas of oral communication which are important in academic life, ie presentations, seminars and tutorials. Chapter 6 focuses on the spoken and written communication skills required for successful networking. Chapter 2 looks at some areas of practical **written communication** in teaching. Another book in this series, *Academic Writing and Referencing for your Education Degree*, explores the writing skills you need to produce academic essays and dissertations.

The word 'communicate' presupposes the involvement of a person or persons on the receiving end of the transmission of information (eg the audience in a presentation) or participating in a two- or multi-way communication process (eg students participating in a seminar or teachers and pupils in school settings). For this reason, some people also use the word **interaction** when discussing these processes.

CROSS
REFERENCE

Academic Writing and Referencing for your Education Degree

CROSS REFERENCE

Studying for your Education Degree, Chapter 3, Becoming a member of your academic and professional community, Graduate attributes

Communicative and interactional competence is the focus of much current educational research (see for example Escobar Urmeneta and Walsh, 2017), and it is seen by many as key in the development of a range of **intellectual and interpersonal skills**. The development of these skills has become increasingly prioritised by universities in recent years. They form an important part of the **'graduate attributes'** promoted by universities, ie the **key transferable skills** which are believed to facilitate academic study while also preparing students for the world of work.

Professional communication

Professional communication is communication that occurs in a professional context rather than a social one. It encompasses pursuing deeper understanding, an open sharing of ideas, the willingness to brainstorm without criticising, and the effective dissemination of information (Cerra and Jacoby, 2003). It requires a high degree of self-awareness and a willingness to understand the lives and experiences of others. This means being aware of the gaps in your knowledge, the things you don't know or understand about the life of a person or people you are talking to. It also involves reflecting on your own values and beliefs. This includes trying to identify and acknowledge your own preconceptions and biases. We all grow up with social and cultural preconceptions and biases, some conscious, some unconscious. Being open to the realities of others and being more aware of your own preconceptions and biases can help you to communicate more sensitively and effectively.

Oral communication

As mentioned earlier, human communication is generally divided into spoken and written communication. Speech, however, is the 'primary form of language' (Barber, 2000, p 2). Speech is learned before writing, and while there are communities that have speech but no written form of their language, no human community has been discovered to have a written language without a spoken one (Barber, 2000). **Oral communication** obviously involves the voice, and the use of **verbal** elements such as sounds, words, phrases and sentences. But it involves much more than these. It comprises **non-verbal** elements such as facial expressions, body language and tone of voice. If you consider talking on the phone or writing an email, you can probably think of difficulties that can arise because of the absence of face-to-face contact with the person you are communicating with. For example, on the phone and in an email, you might need to be very careful when making a joke, as the person on the other end cannot see you smile (though it's perhaps sometimes possible to 'hear' a smile in your tone of voice on the phone). This is why we use 'emojis' ☺ ☹ ☺ in emails and text messages to friends to indicate emotions and pre-empt misunderstandings. However, when this tool is not available, in a more formal email for example, particular care is needed with regard to word choice and phrasing.

Michael Argyle, a renowned social psychologist, identified a number of **non-verbal cues** that humans use when interacting face to face (Argyle, 1988):

- facial expression;
- eye contact;

- posture;
- body space – proximity and closeness to others;
- gesture;
- touch;
- 'artefacts' – clothes and emblems and the way they make us look;
- paralanguage – *how* we say things rather than *what* we say, including intonation (the pitch and melody of the voice), vocal buffers ('oh', 'ah') and vocalisations (laughing, crying, groaning, muttering).

For teachers, it is important to be able to pick up these cues in both children and adults. For example, not noticing or misreading these cues can result in a teacher failing to pick up signs of escalating mental health issues, and this failure could even exacerbate such issues. This is particularly important in areas of primary and secondary education where pupils may be 'emotionally vulnerable' and their learning may be affected by external factors such as biological and environmental factors, early environments and experiences, and interpersonal relationships (Blair and Diamond, 2008; Shankar, 2008).

Communication in education

As a teacher, you will need to communicate with pupils, as well as perhaps their parents, carers and friends. You will also communicate with colleagues: some on a regular basis, others more intermittently. In addition, you will sometimes be required to interact with third parties such as social workers, translators and police officers.

As social beings, we perhaps instinctively feel that communication is an essential part of human relationships. It is generally accepted that interpersonal skills are important and that good communication and interaction should be encouraged in all aspects of life. But your own experience probably tells you that communication can often be tricky, and that people can quite easily misunderstand each other. Look at the following **case studies** and discuss what may have gone wrong, and how, perhaps, miscommunication could possibly have been avoided. Some of the issues raised will be discussed in more detail in later sections of this chapter.

Case studies

A

Aman is sometimes late for the mathematics class. He isn't doing particularly well in his learning in Year 8. Mr George was about 15 minutes into the lesson when Aman appeared at the door. He apologised for being late and was about to sit with his friend when Mr George angrily shouted at him: 'You are late again. The others cannot concentrate on the subject matter because of you. The next time you are late, you will not be allowed to enter the class.'

After the lesson, Aman went to see Mr George in the staffroom. He explained that he was living far from school now, so he had to travel a long way to come to school. He also spoke about his dad losing his job and his family's worsening financial situation. Mr George listened to him without saying a word and then said: 'It makes no difference. These are not valid reasons and you have not apologised. Do not be late again or you will have to bear the consequences.' He ended the conversation, not allowing Aman to say anything further.

1) What are the communication and interpersonal issues here?
2) How should Mr George resolve this communication issue now?

B

On her way to school, Claire often bullies two younger pupils named Francine and Alan. She chases them, pulls their hair, and sometimes takes their breaktime treats. She also makes them steal things from other pupils' desks and give them to her. One day, when she got to school, Claire pushed Alan to the ground because he and Francine did not have any treats to give her. She told them that she would really hurt them if they didn't bring her treats the next day. Alan stood up and tried to push Claire away. The teacher saw them at this point and thought that Alan was the one to blame for the problem. He was sent to detention and was asked to bring his parents to school the next day.

1) What should the teacher have done in this situation?
2) What policies and procedures are normally in place to avoid these sorts of errors of judgement?

C

For years, Alex had been telling her parents that, despite being physically male, she was really a girl. By the time she was 11, she wore only girls' clothes at home or when going out with her family at the weekends. Over the years, her parents came to accept that wearing girls' clothes was very important to Alex and, as strangers they met just seemed to accept Alex was a girl, her parents stopped contradicting them. However, Alex found some things very hard in school: for example, the rule that boys and girls had to wear different uniforms and the way that teachers often divided pupils into separate groups or queues as boys and girls. At age 14, Alex began to ask teachers to use the pronoun 'she' and insisted on wearing a skirt to school. Some pupils started jeering Alex. Some staff automatically and unintentionally referred to Alex as 'he' and 'him' within Alex's earshot. While this upset Alex a little, she said to her teacher: 'At least those who accidentally refer to me as "him" are more genuine than those who say "her" through gritted teeth.'

1) What could make Alex say this? What aspects of paralanguage and body language might she be picking up on?

2) What is most important to Alex regarding the way people talk to or about her?

D

Mary's incident took place in her Year 6 classroom while the pupils were in the room. A father of a boy in her class stormed into her room demanding to speak to her outside the class immediately. Mary asked the father to please step inside because she could not leave her class unattended. The father continued to demand that she come outside. Mary was scared and knew there was no way that she was going to step outside with this irate parent. She felt really panicked. Luckily, another staff member was passing by and saw what was happening. The headteacher was eventually called to resolve the matter.

1) What should the teacher have done in this situation?

2) What procedures and policy are in place to deal with this kind of situation?

Discussion of case studies

A

Mr George wasn't aware of the reasons for Aman's late arrival in his classroom. This lack of information, perhaps combined with his pre-conceived notions about the pupil, led to confrontation and a breakdown in communication. The teacher's behaviour on this occasion conflicts with the requirement in the Teachers' Standards to uphold professionalism in everyday conduct and dealings with pupils (DfE, 2011). Mr George should have carried on with his teaching and spoken to Aman in private, preferably after the lesson, providing an opportunity for him to expand on any external factors affecting attendance or punctuality. The best thing now would probably be for him to apologise to the pupil for the outburst and provide an honest explanation about how individual lateness means that learning is disrupted for everybody. It would be unhelpful for Mr George to be defensive or try to justify his behaviour. He could refer Aman to pastoral care, providing him with support outside the classroom. One simple additional strategy available to the teacher is to leave a few empty chairs near the door for latecomers. There is also the possibility of issuing habitual latecomers with a verbal warning.

B

Schools are legally obliged to tackle bullying, but staff may not always have had the adequate guidance or training to do so effectively. This can mean that attempts to address it often focus on the more obvious forms of bullying, such as physical aggression, while overlooking the views of the pupils involved. Here, the teacher should have consulted with the pupils who appeared to be engaged in bullying and those who appeared to have been victimised in order to learn about the situation. Instead of assuming that Alan was the one bullying Claire, the teacher should have stepped back and attempted to see beyond the 'bully' and 'victim' labels. Before calling parents to school, the teacher should have taken the opportunity to talk with the pupils about what had happened, the likely consequences of their actions, and how they could respond more respectfully next time. Moreover, schools could provide regular sessions to resolve bullying proactively, rather than reacting to specific incidents after the fact.

C

Alex is probably picking up on behaviour which she interprets as negative or judgemental. This is clearly not about what people say, as the people in question are using the language that has been agreed. However, perhaps their tone of voice or facial expression seems to convey that they are not comfortable or happy using this language because they do not understand or accept Alex's identification as female. It is clear that Alex understands that it might be difficult for people to adapt to her situation, and she accepts that people make mistakes; what is important to her is that people are genuine, even if it means showing their doubts or confusion.

D

Mary should have drawn on strategies developed during her professional training. She should have calmly suggested that the father go to the office and speak to someone there. If the situation continued to worsen, she should have contacted somebody to ask for cover for her class and called for her headteacher as a witness. In such heated situations, trying to reason with parents who are upset might not be the best course of action. It might in fact be better to let the person vent their anger and perhaps then try to reason with them in a calm and organised manner.

Communicating with parents and carers

The Teachers' Standards (DfE, 2011) stipulate that a teacher must:

- communicate effectively with parents with regard to pupils' attainment and well-being.

In response to increased expectations, economic pressures and time constraints, Graham-Clay (2005) highlights the need for schools and parents or carers to establish effective partnerships in order to meet the needs of the pupils they 'share'. Epstein (2010) proposed a framework of six major types of involvement which are key to developing a caring relationship between schools and families:

1) parenting;
2) communicating;
3) volunteering;

4) learning at home;

5) decision-making;

6) collaborating with community.

Communication is identified specifically as one of these six types of parent involvement pertinent to establishing strong working relationships between teachers and parents. Communication is also a key factor in the other five areas of involvement.

Positive communication with parents can involve providing suggestions for home conditions which support learning at different key stages. Teachers can provide information and ideas to families about how they can help pupils at home with homework and other curriculum-related activities, including planning and decision-making. This could also involve home visits by teachers at key transition points. Including parents in school decisions means they can be more involved in their children's learning. This could mean helping to develop parent leaders and representatives through active PTAs or other parent organisations. Also, parent-teacher conferences can inform the design of effective forms of school-to-home and home-to-school communications about school programmes and pupils' progress. The following **reflection** touches on some important issues in developing effective parent–teacher communication.

Reflection

1) In what ways do you think communication most affects the parent–teacher relationship?

2) What factors should be considered when talking to parents? (Think about physical, environmental, cultural factors, for example.)

3) What do you need to consider when giving parents information about their children's progress or difficulties in the classroom?

4) Can you think of an incident from your own experience which could have been improved with better communication?

The student-centred learning relationship

Teaching is a complex profession that simultaneously requires practical skills, intellectual skills and interpersonal skills. Communication forms an important part of the latter and, together with appropriate values, it is an essential part of developing a student-centred learning relationship. Lea et al (2003, p 322) suggest that this relationship should be based on the following tenets.

1) A reliance on active instead of passive learning.

2) An interdependence between teacher and learner.

3) Mutual respect within the learner–teacher relationship.

4) A reflexive approach to the teaching and learning process on the part of both teacher and learner.

Good communication between a learner and a teacher is dependent on the establishment of a relationship built on trust and respect and it is underpinned by professional values such as equality of opportunity. Kember (1997) describes two broad orientations in teaching: the teacher-centred/content-oriented conception and the student-centred/learning-oriented conception. Harden and Crosby (2000, p 335) describe teacher-centred learning strategies as having the focus on the teacher, as the expert, transmitting knowledge to the novice. In contrast, student-centred learning focuses on the students' own learning and 'what students do to achieve this, rather than what the teacher does'. Student-centred learning focuses on making students more active in their learning, promoting awareness of what they are doing and why they are doing it. Teachers can use tutorials and discussion groups to promote the inclusion of students in their own learning and assessment. In this learning environment, there is a shift in the locus of power and control so that it is more evenly distributed between the teacher and the learner. This naturally impacts on communication in these settings

Being a good communicator

When speaking to pupils, parents and carers (as well as to other parties), it is essential that you consider the purpose of your communication, ie what you want to achieve. It is important that your communication is clear, meaningful and appropriate, and that the pupil, parent, carer etc is able to process and understand what you say.

The excellent #hellomynameis campaign, led by the late Kate Granger, outlines how simple it can be to improve communication. Although the roots of the campaign lie in health care and nursing, it can be useful in education to improve communication, especially when NQTs or student teachers meet parents or carers for the first time.

It advises that you should do the following.

- Always introduce yourself. In addition, it can be helpful to explain what your role is, eg:

  'Hello, my name is Charlotte [include surname if you wish]. I am a second-year student in teacher training and I will be helping your child to learn and progress in this class.'

- Ask parents and carers (especially older parents or grandparents) how they want to be addressed, eg:

  'Is it OK if I call you Mary?' or 'Do you prefer Mr Khan or Saeed?'

- Check that parents and carers understand what you are saying to them, giving them ample opportunity to ask any questions.

You should also try to avoid:

- technical jargon or difficult language;
- acronyms and abbreviations that you might use as shorthand with other staff members;
- slang;
- terms which might cause offence or convey overfamiliarity.

There are a number of other approaches and strategies which can help you to manage the way you communicate with parents and children, or at least help you to be more aware of the factors which can impact on that communication. Some of these are discussed below.

Communicating feedback in student-centred learning

Feedback is a vital part of learning and positive communication strategies can significantly enhance feedback. Black (1999) identifies some of the difficulties that can present themselves with regard to providing feedback. One point is that teachers may tend to overemphasise communication of marks and grades when talking to pupils while overlooking the learning function of such conversations and the opportunities they afford in terms of providing advice and direction. Another issue is pupils being compared with one another in teacher feedback, thus foregrounding the idea of competition rather than personal improvement.

One important opportunity for positive communication relates to formative assessment. It is argued by many that the inclusion of more formative assessment, which emphasises feedback to pupils on their learning, serves to enhance student learning (Brown et al, 1997; Light and Cox, 2001, p 170). By developing more formative assessment for inclusion in courses, teachers can provide a clear focus for the pupil by highlighting their learning gaps and areas that they can develop. Providing oral feedback (instead of or in addition to written feedback) on assessment tasks such as essays and presentations can help to engage students in their learning, especially if a dialogic approach is adopted.

Providing individual feedback is an important part of teaching. However, it is also important to remember that, as a teacher, it is your responsibility to promote learning in all the children in your class. Simon (1999) alerts us to the danger of focusing completely on the individual learner and losing sight of the needs of the whole class when communicating feedback to pupils.

Black and Wiliam (2009, p 8) emphasise some key strategies for communicating effective formative feedback which covers the needs of the individual and the whole class.

1) Clarifying, sharing and promoting understanding of learning intentions and criteria for success.

2) Providing feedback that moves students forward.

3) Activating students as instructional resources for one another.

4) Activating students as the owners of their own learning.

It is important that feedback draws attention to the positive elements of the students' performance and that the targets set are clearly communicated to the students. Feedback can also include constructive criticism: advice that provokes students to improve task performance.

Reflection

> Is the feedback below likely to enhance student learning? Why/Why not?
>
> 1) 'You did a brilliant job. You're very smart.'
> 2) 'Your presentation was poor. Put more effort in next time.'
> 3) 'You are describing yourself here. You were supposed to analyse the problem.'
>
> Can you think of some alternative ways of expressing genuine interest in and concern for the pupils' progress and learning?

Discussion of reflection

1) 'You did a brilliant job. You're very smart.'

Feedback of this nature runs the risk of reinforcing a fixed mindset. Compare this with:

> 'You did a brilliant job. Your original strategy didn't work, but you tried another approach which worked well.'

Here the focus is on the process of learning, something which students can take concrete action to improve upon. Students can be derailed by the idea of fixed, immutable abilities (adapted from Dweck, 2007).

2) 'Your presentation was poor. Put more effort in next time.'

This sounds dismissive and there is no attempt to provide clear direction or identify future goals. Compare this with:

> 'Well done. Your presentation skills have improved. To improve further still, you need to develop the use of your teaching voice and don't forget to make regular eye contact with your audience. Try these two things next time round and let's see if you can make the form team.'

3) 'You are describing yourself here. You were supposed to analyse the problem.'

This is wholly negative and fails to signpost how the pupil can improve. Compare with:

> 'That's a detailed description. Move on to the explanation earlier, as it is also important. You've named places, but think about how you could compare them.'

Egan's Skilled Helper Model

Teachers often have pastoral responsibilities which include helping students help themselves. Egan's Skilled Helper Model (2002) can be a particularly useful framework for this purpose, and it is founded on good communication skills.

The model has three stages which can be summarised as:

- Exploration – what is going on?
- Challenging – what do I want instead?
- Action planning – how might I achieve what I want?

Stage 1: Exploration

The first task is to find out your student's story, to elicit from them what is happening in their own words, and then to reflect it back to them, without judgement.

This may involve:

- attention giving – positive body language, eye contact, etc;
- active listening – leaning forward, nodding, focusing on what is being said rather than what you plan to say in response (active listening is discussed in more detail in the following section);
- acceptance and empathy – it is vital to detach from your judgement about what you are being told;
- paraphrasing and summarising – to check your own understanding of what has been said.

Stage 2: Challenging

This stage involves challenging existing views – one issue at a time. Encourage the pupil to think about whether there is another way of looking at the issue.

Some useful questions via which to do this are:

- What might this look like from another person's point of view?
- What in particular about this is a problem for you?

Stage 3: Action planning

Since the object is to achieve lasting change and to empower pupils to manage their own problems more effectively and develop unused opportunities more fully, developing an action plan for the future is key.

Useful questions here include:

- What are the possible ways forward in this situation?
- Which of these feel best for you?

Your goal as an effective communicator is to turn good intentions into actual results, so it is important to help your pupil to set realistic, practical and achievable targets.

(adapted from the University of Glasgow, based on Egan, 2002)

Active listening

A well-known strategy believed to aid communication in contexts such as teaching is active listening. By definition, the term 'active listening' challenges the idea that listening is a passive process in which one person (the speaker) 'does something' and the other person (the listener) simply 'absorbs' information. The process of 'active' listening involves paying close attention to the person speaking, noticing the words they use, their tone of voice, their facial expression and their body language, and reflecting on what all of this conveys about what they are thinking and how they are feeling. It requires you to be 'present' in the moment (Rogers, 1961), to listen carefully and show genuine interest, and to make every attempt to understand the point of view of the person you are talking to, be they a pupil, parent, carer or colleague.

Active listening is used widely in healthcare and can be very useful in other public-facing professions like teaching. It involves the following (adapted from Jagger et al, 2015):

- Verbal communication, for example:
  - acknowledging what the other person is saying, and signalling your own reflective state, often by using words such as 'yes', 'right', 'I see', or even recognisable sounds such as 'ah' and 'uh um';
  - clarification techniques such as checking that you have interpreted the speaker's message correctly or using direct questioning;
  - restating, paraphrasing or summarising the speaker's message to check understanding and provide a focus.
- Non-verbal communication, for example:
  - non-verbal aspects of 'paralanguage', such as intonation;
  - body language, such as posture, eye contact, facial expressions, gestures and touch;
  - being quiet and perhaps still, creating space for the other person to think and express themselves.

Active listening is important in teaching for a number of reasons.

- It can help teachers in their assessment of pupils' needs.
- It is an effective way of conveying the genuine concern and interest that a teacher should have for a pupil's progress and learning.
- It can support pupils and parents who find it difficult to express themselves in what may seem to them to be a stressful situation.
- It can help teachers to manage a volatile or highly emotional situation.
- It can help teachers to know when and how to engage with a pupil, and to respond in the right way, be it through eye contact, a knowing look or a smile.

Task

Identify some active listening techniques employed by teachers in the following exchanges with pupils or parents.

1)

Pupil: 'Some days I can read for my homework quite easily. Then other days my mind is quite distracted and I don't stick to what I need to do.'

Teacher: 'Uh um, so your time management varies from day to day.'

2)

Pupil: 'There are days when I just can't face coming to school. You can't imagine what it feels like.'

Teacher: 'So, when you have these days, can you try to explain to me more what it feels like?'

3)

Parent: 'My son has been diagnosed with diabetes and has to start taking medication.'

Teacher: 'Do you have any more information about what type of diabetes it is – type 1 or type 2? Do you know what medication is he on? Does he need to take anything in school?'

Parent: 'Yes, I have brought the medication with me.'

Teacher: 'Let's see if we can arrange a meeting with the school nurse.'

4)

Teacher: 'Tell me a bit more about how you spend your time when you go home in the evenings. When do you finish your homework? Do you have a separate room for that?'

Pupil: 'Well it's not good, especially since we moved to a new house. Mum said that the council would soon give us a bigger house but at the moment we don't have enough bedrooms for all my brothers and sisters. I do my homework at a table under the stairs.'

Teacher: 'Would you like me to help you with this problem? What do you want to change in your situation? Would you like to finish your homework in the homework club here at school?'

Questioning techniques

It is impossible to carry out a thorough assessment of an issue without asking questions. Most of these questions will be routine, but it's likely that you will at some point have to ask pupils and other people difficult questions. Depending on the situation, you may have to ask questions related to issues such as home and family relationships, parental support, time management and mental health. Where the safeguarding of a child or vulnerable young adult is an issue, you will have no choice but to ask these sorts of questions.

In general terms, it is worth being aware of the different types of question you might ask – both with difficult questions and the more routine ones – and to consider how appropriate or effective each type may be in a given situation.

The three main types of question in English are discussed below.

Closed questions

These are questions such as:

> 'Did you get to school on time?'
> 'Have you spoken to your form tutor?'

They anticipate an answer of 'yes' or 'no' and are therefore sometimes referred to as 'yes/no questions'. Closed questions are useful as conversation openers as they make it easy for the other person to answer, and they don't force them to reveal too much about themselves. They are also particularly useful when you need information quickly in order to establish facts, for example in an emergency situation. However, be aware of inadvertently asking closed questions which may be seen as leading questions.

Open questions

These are questions such as:

> 'How long have you been experiencing this problem?'
> 'Why did you not talk to me earlier about this issue?'

They usually begin with a 'question word' such as 'what/where/when/who/why/how', and are sometimes known as 'wh-questions'. They do not presuppose a particular answer, and they can elicit both long and short answers, eg:

> Teacher: 'What is the nature of the problem?'
> Pupil: 'Can't concentrate.'
> 'It's difficult to talk about. I can't concentrate on school work or sleep at night because of my stepfather partying with his mates for hours at night.'

Open questions can be used to follow up on closed questions to elicit additional conversations. They are also particularly good for initiating conversations about difficult topics:

> Teacher: 'I am sorry to hear that. Have you spoken to your mum about it? Do you want me to speak to her?'

Searching/Probing questions

Probing questions are useful if we are looking for more information or developing critical thinking behaviour in our pupils. They are less specific than open questions and provide space to get pupils talking about their personal opinions and feelings, for example:

'What exactly did you mean by …?'
'Could you tell me more about this?'

Probing questions are good as follow-on questions to check that a pupil is giving a full and accurate account because you can probe for more detail and check against other information you may have, for example:

'How do you know that is true?'
'How does that compare with what you said before?'

Reflection

Think about how you might phrase questions when you need to find out about a pupil's:

- lack of concentration in lessons;

- continuous absence from school;

- behaviour issues in the playground.

Everyday communication in the classroom

Language and communication skills are both the foundation and fundamental building blocks for learning. Just the way teachers talk with pupils every day can influence learning, memory, understanding and the motivation to learn. The quality of spoken dialogue in classrooms can significantly improve children's educational attainment and behaviour for learning.

The Communication Commitment (2019), developed by The Communication Trust and based on the Ofsted framework, provides some useful guidance here.

- Measuring and improving pupils' communication skills: 'No Pens Day Wednesday' – a day focusing completely on speaking and listening is a useful resource for incorporating effective communication into daily teaching.

- Quality of teaching in school: include clear ways to assess and measure the quality of teaching of communication skills in your school.

- Behaviour and safety of pupils at school: encourage pupils to become 'Communication Ambassadors'. More information is available through the Communication Trust's fact sheet *Empowering Children and Young People to Become Communication Ambassadors.*

Positivity

It is extremely important to connect with your pupils in a positive way. Pupils of all ages want to feel that their teachers like them and want the best for them. The Communication Commitment and the Ofsted Framework (2019) draw on a growing body of evidence on the links between positive communication strategies and good behaviour. For all pupils, positive behaviour is often built upon effective social communication skills and clear understanding. Moreover, positive communication is central to Teachers' Standard 7 (DfE, 2011), which expects teachers to manage behaviour effectively to ensure a good and safe learning environment. This can involve the following: using a kind voice when speaking to pupils; listening to all of your pupils; encouraging pupils to share ideas and opinions; if pupils have done something positive, sharing it with the rest of the class; encouraging community spirit; and when a pupil speaks to you, stopping and genuinely listening.

Being human!

The frameworks, strategies and techniques outlined above can be very helpful. Even if you don't adopt them systematically and completely, familiarity with them can still help make you more aware of the issues involved when you are communicating with pupils and parents. As you might expect, emerging as they do from fundamental teaching and learning principles, they share much common ground. They prioritise certain values and attributes such as respect, empathy, equality of opportunity, genuineness and student-centred teaching and learning. However, it can sometimes be challenging to follow the requirements of these frameworks in certain situations. It can also be difficult to hold multiple considerations in your head at the same time while remaining natural, present and 'human' in your interaction. If you do feel a bit awkward or overwhelmed, it is perhaps a good idea to start with trying to focus on some simple communicational principles as outlined in the following **top tips** box.

Top tips

Keeping it simple

- **Pay attention** to the person you are speaking to and **listen** to what they say. This should go a long way towards helping you achieve positive outcomes. Paying attention and listening should, for example, help you pick up on the perspective and feelings of your pupils.

- Teachers' Standard 8 (DfE, 2011) expects teachers to **communicate effectively** with parents with regard to pupils' achievements and well-being. When you speak and ask/answer questions, the important thing is to **make yourself understood** to the pupils or parents, using simple words and short sentences where possible. Give them the time and the opportunity to process information and make sure you **check** that they have done so. This includes taking account of those pupils or parents whose first language is not English, or who may have a disability which affects communication. It is also a consideration if English is not your own first language: don't worry about minor grammar mistakes or the fact that you have an accent (everyone has an accent – a French accent, a South African accent, an American accent, a southern English accent, a Mancunian accent, etc); focus on being clear.

- **Put genuine interest in your pupils' welfare at the heart of your communication and interaction with pupils and parents.** Active listening goes a long way in helping pupils and parents feel that the teacher is not only listening to their concerns but also understanding the root causes. It is important to reflect on the situation and any accompanying feelings in order to fully communicate with pupils and parents. The accuracy of the situation and accompanying feelings can then be confirmed by both parties involved. This provides active engagement and helps both the teacher and pupils/parents to gain a better understanding of the situation.

Here are some other **top tips** to help you in particular education contexts.

Top tips

Conducting parent conferences

When preparing for parent conferences, note the following.

- Parent and staff vulnerabilities: having a sound understanding of vulnerabilities that both parents (and staff) can feel when communicating can help teachers to reflect on how best to achieve a positive outcome.

- Strengths-based approach: focusing on strengths and not just negative aspects of the pupil helps in establishing trust with parents and convincing them that teachers have the best interests of their child at heart.

- Essential communication skills: ensuring that your communication is as clear and positive for the other person as you think it is.

- Common communication mistakes: understanding common mistakes that hinder communication can help prevent them from happening.

- Cultural differences: being aware that cultural differences may affect communication can help teachers prepare.

(Department of Health, 2019)

Top tips

Completing forms

If using a standard form in school, try to make the information-gathering exercise more like a **natural conversation** rather than a questionnaire. This will help you build up **rapport** with the pupil. It might be important that all of the questions on the form are asked but they need not be in the order listed or necessarily asked exactly as written. Make use of additional reflecting ('So, let me just check…') and probing statements ('Tell me a bit more about that…') to ensure that the information is accurate.

Top tips

Delivering critical feedback

It is always difficult to deliver critical feedback to pupils. It is important that pupils understand that you have their best interests at heart, even when you are being critical, and this requires an atmosphere of trust. This can be created in small ways over time:

- remember and use pupils' names;
- develop a habit of noticing pupils' positive attributes and acknowledging them in class;
- acknowledge student successes, even small ones;
- show genuine interest in the answers pupils give to your questions;
- listen carefully to your pupils' questions and concerns;
- smile, laugh and share jokes when appropriate.

Developing good communication skills through practice and feedback

If you are reading this book, it is hopefully because you believe it can help you to improve your communication skills. This book aims to raise your awareness of the issues involved and strategies that you may find helpful. However, this book, or any other book, is only part of the story. As with any skill, the best way to improve is through **practice** (Figure 1.1). This is the case whether you are learning an academic or professional skill, or whether you are learning a new language or how to dance the tango. And for practice to be truly effective, it needs to be accompanied by **feedback** (Figure 1.1), ie advice on how you can improve in the future.

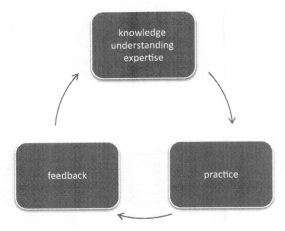

Figure 1.1: The learning cycle

As a student teacher, you will receive feedback from lecturers, mentors, peers and parents and carers. In order to benefit from feedback, you should be aware of how to interpret it and use it. You should approach feedback in a positive manner, with the intention to reflect on it seriously and carefully – there is always room for improvement, no matter how experienced a person is. Focus on both strengths and weaknesses, and try to identify small steps that you can take to improve in one or two specific areas – you can't put everything right at once. As a student teacher, you will be supervised in many aspects of your training. However, if you realise that you feel uncomfortable or lacking in confidence in a particular area of practice, you should actively seek supervision so that you can obtain the feedback you need in order to improve.

CROSS
REFERENCE

*Studying
for your
Education
Degree,*
Chapter 6,
Assessment,
Feedback on
academic
work

Role-play

One way of practising your communication skills on your degree programme is through **role-play**. People have different reactions to role-play, but it is an established part of many education degree programmes, so you need to be able to participate in it effectively. It is therefore worthwhile reflecting on how you feel about role-play and how you can best approach it if you find it difficult.

Reflection

1) What experience have you had of role-play?
2) Which of the following would you associate with your experience of role-play? Why?

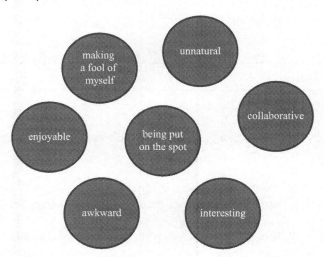

3) If you chose some or mostly negative associations, consider how you might adopt a more positive approach. You could start by recognising that role-play is designed to test out situations in a safe environment; it is better to make mistakes in role-play and learn from them than it is to be overconfident with real pupils.

Communicating with others

As noted earlier in the chapter, as a teacher, you will have to communicate with a range of people in addition to pupils and their talk to parents or carers, both informally and in more formal contexts. You will also communicate with colleagues and third parties such as other members of the childcare team, social workers, educational psychologists, translators or local authorities.

The Teachers' Standards detail a number of professional responsibilities which are in many ways dependent on good communication with a range of professional colleagues.

A teacher must:

- make a positive contribution to the wider life and ethos of the school;
- develop effective professional relationships with colleagues, knowing how and when to draw on advice and specialist support;
- take responsibility for improving teaching through appropriate professional development, responding to advice and feedback from colleagues.

Summary

This chapter has explored the role of oral communication in education, including both verbal and non-verbal features. It has examined the role of oral communication in the classroom and school environment and presented some approaches, strategies and techniques which could help you to communicate more clearly, appropriately and effectively with pupils and other parties.

References

Argyle, M (1988) *Bodily Communication*. 2nd ed. London: Methuen.

Barber, C (2000) *The English Language*. Canto edition. Cambridge: Cambridge University Press.

Black, P (1999) Assessment, Learning Theories and Testing Systems. In Murphy, J (ed) *Learners, Learning and Assessment*. London: Open University Press.

Black, P and Wiliam, D (2009) Developing the Theory of Formative Assessment. *Educational Assessment, Evaluation and Accountability*, 21(1): 5–31 [online]. Available at: https://kclpure.kcl.ac.uk/portal/files/9119063/Black2009_Developing_the_theory_of_formative_assessment.pdf (accessed 26 February 2019).

Blair, C and Diamond, A (2008) Biological Processes in Prevention and Intervention: The Promotion of Self-Regulation as a Means of Preventing School Failure. *Development and Psychopathology*, 20: 899–911.

Brown, G, Bull, J and Pendlebury, M (1997) What is Assessment? *Assessing Student Learning in Higher Education*. London: Routledge.

Cerra, C and Jacoby, R (2003) *Teacher Talk! The Art of Effective Communication* (School Talk series). San Francisco: Jossey-Bass (USA).

Communication Trust (2019) Communication Commitment [online]. Available at: www.thecommunicationtrust.org.uk/projects/communication-commitment/ (accessed 18 April 2019).

Department for Education (2011) Teachers' Standards [online]. Available at: www.gov.uk/government/uploads/system/uploads/attachment_data/file/665520/Teachers__Standards.pdf (accessed 26 February 2019).

Department of Health (2019) Be You: Communicating with Parents, Mind Matters [online]. Available at: https://beyou.edu.au/about-be-you (accessed 19 June 2019).

Dweck, C S (2007) The Perils and Promises of Praise. *ASCD*, 65(12): 34–9 [online]. Available at: www.ascd.org/publications/educational-leadership/oct07/vol65/num02/The-Perils-and-Promises-of-Praise.aspx (accessed 26 February 2019).

Egan, G (2002) *The Skilled Helper: A Problem Management and Opportunity Development Approach to Helping*. 7th ed. Pacific Grove, CA: Brooks Cole.

Egan, G (2006) *Essentials of Skilled Helping: Managing Problems, Developing Opportunities*. Pacific Grove, CA: Brooks Cole.

Epstein, J L (2010) School/Family/Community Partnerships: Caring for the Children We Share. *Phi Delta Kappan*, 92(3) [online]. Available at: https://doi.org/10.1177/003172171009200326 (accessed 26 February 2019).

Escobar Urmeneta, C and Walsh, S (2017) Classroom Interactional Competence in Content and Language Integrated Learning. In Llinares, A and Morton, T (eds) *Applied Linguistic Perspectives on CLIL* (pp 189–206). Amsterdam: John Benjamins.

Graham-Clay, S (2005) Communicating with Parents: Strategies for Teachers. *School Community Journal*, 15(1): 117–29 [online]. Available at: https://eric.ed.gov/?id=EJ794819 (accessed 26 February 2019).

Harden, R M and Crosby, J (2000) AMEE Guide No 20: The Good Teacher Is More Than a Lecturer – the Twelve Roles of the Teacher. *Medical Teacher*, 22(4): 334–47 [online]. Available at: http://njms.rutgers.edu/education/office_education/community_preceptorship/documents/TheGoodTeacher.pdf (accessed 26 February 2019).

Hellomynameis [online]. Available at: www.hellomynameis.org.uk (accessed 28 April 2019).

Jagger, C, Iles-Smith, H and Jones, J (2015) Nursing Therapeutics. In Burns, D (ed) *Foundations of Adult Nursing* (pp 35–62). London: Sage.

Kember, D (1997) A Reconceptualisation of the Research into University Academics' Conceptions of Teaching. *Learning and Instruction*, 7(3): 255–75 [online]. Available at: www.sciencedirect.com/science/article/pii/S095947529600028X (accessed 26 February 2019).

Lea, S J, Stephenson, D and Troy, J (2003) Higher Education Students' Attitudes to Student Centred Learning: Beyond 'educational bulimia'. *Studies in Higher Education* 28(3): 321–34.

Light, G and Cox, R (2001) Assessing: Student Assessment. *Learning and Teaching in Higher Education: The Reflective Practitioner.* London: Paul Chapman Publishing.

O'Neill, G, Moore, S and McMullin, B (2005) Student-Centred Learning: What Does it Mean for Students and Lecturers? In *Emerging Issues in the Practice of University Learning and Teaching.* Dublin. *Aishe* [online]. Available at: www.ucd.ie/teaching/t4media/Student%20Centered%20Learning%20Article.pdf (accessed 26 February 2019).

Rogers, C (1961) *On Becoming a Person: A Therapist's View of Psychotherapy.* London: Redwood Books.

Shanker, S (2008) In Search of the Pathways That Lead to Mentally Healthy Children. *Journal of Developmental Processes*, 3(1): 22–3 [online]. Available at: file:///C:/Users/kulwinder/Downloads/In_Search_of_the_Pathways_that_Lead_to_Mentally_He.pdf (accessed 26 February 2019).

Simon, B (1999) *Why no pedagogy in England?* In Leach, J and Moon, B (eds) *Learners and Pedagogy.* London: Sage Publications.

Chapter 2
Professional writing skills

Learning outcomes

After reading this chapter you will:

- have developed an understanding of a range of professional writing contexts in education;

- be aware of how to follow the guidelines contained in the Teachers' Standards and those typical of school policies;

- be better able to write clear, well-organised reports;

- be better able to write official correspondence;

- be aware of how to produce effective information leaflets.

This chapter will help you to understand the kind of writing that is expected of you as a professional educator. It will help you to achieve different writing goals and to develop your professional writing skills.

Writing basics

When writing any text, the key considerations are **audience** and **purpose**.

- Who will be reading the text?
- What is your purpose in writing the text?

With respect to academic essay writing, the concepts of audience and purpose are explored in detail in another book in this series, *Academic Writing and Referencing for your Education Degree*. Audience and purpose should also guide the writing that you need to do as part of your teaching practice. This includes record keeping, writing reports, developing parent information leaflets (for example, giving guidance on helping children with reading), and writing correspondence such as letters and emails to parents and carers, statutory/non-statutory agencies or other education professionals. Each of these will be discussed in more detail below.

CROSS REFERENCE

Academic Writing and Referencing for your Education Degree, Chapter 1, Academic writing: text, process and criticality, Approaching a writing assignment

Written communication and record keeping in schools

Good written communication, including good record keeping, is essential for teachers. Teachers need to be able to communicate in written form in a way which is clear and appropriate. They need to maintain clear, accurate records related to attendance, records of work, progress, assessment, safeguarding etc. For trainee teachers, in particular, it is important to develop writing skills related to lesson planning and reflections on teaching, as well as commentaries on progress towards achieving each of the Teachers' Standards (DfE, 2011). One particular point of the Teachers' Standards makes direct reference to standards of literacy.

A teacher must:

- demonstrate an understanding of and take responsibility for promoting high standards of literacy, articulacy and the correct use of standard English, whatever the teacher's specialist subject.

Schools have their own policies on communication based around the Teachers Standards. The example below, devised by St Michael's C of E Primary School in Bishop Middleham, encompasses much of what is considered good practice in both oral and written communication.

Effective communication

- Enhances the interest and satisfaction of all members of staff in their work.
- Promotes a general feeling of partnership between parents, school and community.
- Generates confidence and pride in the work of the school.
- Improves the effectiveness of the school.
- Enables all staff to engage in and contribute to the management of the school.
- Creates a positive culture for learning.

The school provides the following guidelines.

- The circulation of relevant information, both from within and outside the school, is accurate, timely, sensitively transmitted and accompanied by explanation.
- Decisions concerning the circulation of information and concerning consultation are made in accordance with the school's equal opportunities policy.
- All interactions should be open, honest, positive and show respect for others.
- Conduct is consistent with our written values.
- Information regarding individuals which needs to be communicated to others is made known to the individual concerned.

- All staff are responsible for effective communication in all aspects of their work.
- Confidentiality must be respected.
- Written communications with parents and other external contacts must comply with agreed practice.
- Consultation issues, plans and changes which may affect the work of the school are inclusive of all appropriate stakeholder groups.

.ook at the following **case studies** relating to written communication practices and :onsider what would be good practice in each case.

Case studies

A

Ian works at a school in which it is policy that written parental reports are produced once a year and issued at parents' evenings. The following is his report for a student he has now taught for just over half of the academic year.

So far this year, students have covered topics including number, shape and data. For the data topic, we went on a class trip to the high street, where we surveyed members of the public using questionnaires we had designed; we then made graphs and charts using our data.

Aimee's group made a fantastic display for the data project. Aimee also made a beautiful tessellation during the 'shape' topic, and her score in the recent assessment was 72 per cent. Well done Aimee!

B

Ivan also works at Ian's school. The following is his report for a student, again written mid-way through the year.

Barry is a polite student who is a pleasure to teach. Barry always completes homework on time and to a good standard. Barry has done well in number but struggled in data.

To improve, they should:

- practice times tables for the weekly test;
- use the MyMaths website to help with any topics they find difficult;
- ensure all homework is completed.

C

Iain's school produces summative reports, issued at the end of the academic year. Of one of his students, he writes the following.

Cai joined the class at Christmas and has been a very negative influence on the group. He seems to think it appropriate to make foolish noises while I am trying to teach the class, and relishes the attention that his unacceptable behaviour attracts. It seems clear that he has ADHD.

I hope very much that Cai will start acting his age next year, so that he can stop ruining the education of both himself and his classmates, but I regret to report that he has, this year, been unteachable.

D

Iwan has logged a case on his school's safeguarding reporting system, after one of his students came to see him after a lesson.

Dora stayed back at breaktime this morning and asked if she could speak to me. She has been uncharacteristically withdrawn for a couple of weeks now, and while on duty outside, I have observed her staying by herself, where previously she would play with a clique of friends; her work has also suffered during this period.

Dora was reluctant to speak, but after I reassured her, she eventually disclosed that she is being emotionally abused by her older sister, who has recently moved back to her family home. This has been going on for almost a month, and has left her feeling very unhappy and uncomfortable around other people, particularly girls.

Her friends, unaware of the reason for her change, have interpreted her behaviour as being stand-offish, and one girl, who she asked me not to name, has been posting hurtful comments on Facebook; this girl has also started posting images in which she has photoshopped Dora's head onto upsetting images, and Dora has seen other students looking at these on their phones.

Discussion of case studies

A

Given that it has been written part-way through the year, Ian's report should be at least partially formative in nature.

Although Ian praises Aimee's work, his comments are entirely concerned with its aesthetics, rather than its value as evidence of her ability or learning. The only reference to Aimee's achievement in the report is that she achieved a test score of 72 per cent, but without context, this means little – he does not state what was being assessed, nor does he give any suggestions about what she can do to progress.

B

Ivan opens his report with comments which suggest an individually prepared report, but his points for improvement appear impersonal and generic. The use of the plural pronoun 'they' suggests that the comments have been written to be copied and pasted for all students rather than written specifically for Barry (although it could be argued that 'they' can be used as a singular pronoun – see below); this is reinforced by the inclusion of the target to ensure homework is completed, when Barry has actually been praised for his homework at the start of the report.

While a certain amount of 'bulk' writing of comments may be commonplace, and often appropriate, if it is apparent to a parent or carer that their child's comments have been prepared without individual consideration, this can lead to these comments being disregarded, even though they may contain useful, relevant information.

In the report, Ivan misspells the verb 'practice' ('practise' is the verb in UK English, eg practise your tables; 'practice' is a noun, eg attending football practice). As previously noted, the Teachers' Standards require teachers to 'take responsibility for promoting high standards of literacy, articulacy and the correct use of standard English'. However, notions of standard English can be problematic and controversial. It is perhaps fairly uncontroversial to object to spelling mistakes as spelling rules are generally agreed (though there are accepted variations) and words can after all be checked in a dictionary. But not all language issues are so simple. Some people, including parents, may for instance object to the possible use of 'they' in Ivan's report as a singular pronoun. It is impossible to please everyone in cases such as this, but teachers should be aware of the various debates surrounding 'correct' or prescribed usage so that they can respond knowledgeably if challenged. On the matter of the use of 'they', the Oxford English Dictionary blog page has an interesting summary of the history and debate surrounding usage (including the historical precedent of singular usage) by a Professor of Language and Linguistics at the University of Illinois (Baron, 2018). Baron reaches a conclusion which, even though somewhat light-hearted, will, as is always the case in these matters, divide people: he believes those who oppose singular usage of 'they' are fighting a losing battle:

'Even people who object to singular they as a grammatical error use it themselves when they're not looking'.

However, in this case, it is important to remember that the main problem with the use of 'they' is the fact that it seems to indicate generic rather than individual feedback.

C

Whatever else one might think of his report, Iain can, at least, not be accused of writing a generic report. This is, however, unlikely to be a helpful report for Cai's parents. The report makes no mention of Cai's attainment, progress or, indeed, education, except to label him 'unteachable', and it reads as an attack on the child rather than a communication between school and parents.

While it may be appropriate to mention behaviour in a report, there is a balance to be struck; criticising the child in this way is unlikely to get parents onside, particularly as the report is devoid of positives. It also seems improbable that Cai's parents would be unaware of his behavioural issues, particularly if they have been ongoing for half of the academic year. Iain also uses the acronym ADHD in his report. Quite apart from the fact that the diagnosis seems to come from Iain himself and is a supposition, the use of the acronym is unhelpful since parents may be unaware of what it means.

D

Iwan states that he has observed a number of changes in Dora for several weeks, any one of which could have been symptomatic of a concern, but makes no mention of having reported these.

In the second paragraph, Iwan gives his interpretation of Dora's disclosure, rather than her words, and the phrase 'emotionally abused' is far too broad a term for the person acting upon his statement to understand clearly what has taken place. His later reference to 'upsetting' images is also ambiguous.

Iwan later describes bullying by another student but says that he's agreed not to name the perpetrator. He should have made it clear to Dora that he could not promise secrecy, since he is obliged to report any disclosures concerning criminal activity or abuse of a child in his care.

Top tips

> **Writing student reports**
>
> - Avoid acronyms and abbreviations or giving the term in full to accompany the short form;
> - Avoid phrasing which is esoteric and therefore exclusive, eg 'Harry presents with features of dyslexia';
> - Ensure that information and opinions are sensitively transmitted and accompanied by explanation.

Use and misuse of abbreviations and acronyms

When communicating with fellow professionals, abbreviations and acronyms which are familiar to all parties can provide a helpful shortcut and reduce text length. However, the use of abbreviations should be considered carefully when communicating with people who might not readily understand them.

It is important to balance speed (abbreviations and acronyms save time) with accuracy and transparency.

Note:

An **acronym** is the short form of a multi-word term, often a proper name. Acronyms are usually formed by using the first letter of each word, but they are sometimes adapted slightly to make them more readable or memorable. Examples include:

BBC (British Broadcasting Corporation)

PEACH (Parents for the Early Intervention of Autism in Children)

An **abbreviation** is formed by simply shortening a word; this is usually indicated by a full stop. Examples include:

approx. (approximately)

etc. (from the Latin *et cetera*)

Task

1) What do the abbreviations and acronyms below stand for?

2) Which of them are acceptable in record keeping and report writing and which are best avoided? Give reasons.

eg	**SEND**	**Ofsted**	**WALT**
SATs	**SENCO**	**ADHD**	**SSP**

Discussion of task

eg – acceptable

This means 'for example' and is commonly used in both professional and everyday writing. The letters 'eg' actually stand for the Latin 'exempli gratia', which would be an unacceptable form to use as it might be unfamiliar to readers and has connotations of exclusivity.

SATs – acceptable

Standard Assessment Tasks are used for national curriculum assessment and were previously known as Standard Assessment Tests. Most people are familiar with the acronym, but it might be wise to include the term in full when it is initially used in a document.

SEND – best avoided

SEND (Special Educational Needs and Disabilities) refers to learning difficulties for which special educational provision has to be made. Apart from potential confusion for readers, because 'send' is a common word, the term is rather esoteric and, while commonly used in education, may be unfamiliar to people who do not work in the profession.

SENCO – best avoided

The SENCO (SEN Co-ordinator) is the teacher responsible for co-ordinating SEND provision in a school and for ensuring that students with learning difficulties, emotional problems and behavioural problems receive appropriate support, as well as overseeing the completion of Individual Education Plans (IEPs) and liaising with external agencies. For parents whose children have an IEP, the SENCO is an important point of contact, but the acronym may prove confusing, at least for initial communications.

Ofsted – acceptable

Ofsted (the Office for Standards in Education, Children's Services and Skills) inspects education and training and is widely known outside education circles. However, as with other terms, fuller details might be given when the acronym is first used in a communication.

ADHD – not acceptable

ADHD (Attention Deficit Hyperactive Disorder) refers to a particular diagnosed condition which affects behaviour. It is complex and requires explanation when used, so is best avoided until concerned parties are familiar with it.

WALT – best avoided

WALT tells children what 'We Are Learning Today' and is familiar to children in schools where the term is commonplace. It might be used with parents once they are familiar with its meaning.

SSP – best avoided

Although widely understood in primary schools to refer to an approach to teaching reading, Systemic Synthetic Phonics*, SSP has three possible meanings: (1) Systematic Synthetic Phonics; (2) Starting Salary Point; (3) Safer School Partnership. As there is more than one interpretation, it is advisable to use the full term to avoid ambiguity and confusion. Moreover, the phonics-related meaning requires explanation for people who do not work in primary education, another reason to use the full term rather than the acronym.

*The 'synthetic' part of the term refers to the part played by synthesising (blending) the letters of words from left to right, and sounding them to blend (synthesise) the sounds to words. For example, if children see the word 'cat', they would sound each grapheme as a phoneme (c–a–t).

For an excellent guide to acronyms and abbreviations in education, see Hickman (2013).

Avoiding jargon

When you habitually use certain technical terms including abbreviations and acronyms, it can be hard to put yourself in the shoes of someone who does not have the same technical knowledge as you. This could apply to someone outside your professional community, or even a colleague who has not been working in the same area as you.

Task

Improve the notes made by a SENCO on a pupil, taking into account the comments and guidance provided in previous sections.

Faisal presents with elements of dyslexia and finds learning many basic GPCs in SSP lessons challenging. There are indications of ADHD. Suggest HSLO make contact with parents pdq.

Confidentiality

You are probably aware of new legislation on data protection. If you have been in employment or volunteering for a charity, you have probably been asked to complete training to bring you up to date with this legislation; and if you use the internet, you cannot fail to have noticed that the number of boxes you are required to tick has been on the up. This is because, on 25 May 2018, the EU General Data Protection Regulation (GDPR) came into force alongside a new UK Data Protection Act. This new legislation is concerned with 'person identifying information' (PII), such as a person's name and address, and the way this information is collected, stored and used. The legislation requires that organisations and individuals:

- collect and retain only the minimum amount of PII data necessary;
- are transparent with people about how they are using their data;
- provide people with choices with regard to this usage where possible;
- keep the data they collect secure;
- retain data only for as long as it is required.

As a trainee teacher, you will be required to follow data protection guidelines issued by your host university and your placement school. In particular, you need to be aware that breaches of GDPR can have serious financial consequences (big fines) for the organisations involved. While many breaches are accidental, part of the reasoning behind GDPR was to try to force organisations (through big fines) to ensure their staff take the processing of PII more seriously. Few data protection breaches in education are a result of criminality or downright negligence; most are in fact down to carelessness, eg:

- leaving confidential paperwork in unattended places like on a desk in an unlocked office;
- leaving an unencrypted electronic device with personal information on it in unattended places, eg losing your mobile with work email on a bus;
- emailing personal information to the wrong person, eg sending an email reply to all rather than a single recipient;
- sending a letter to the wrong address;
- posting pictures or information on social media without checking for personal information, eg photos of colleagues with children visible in the background.

Such lapses can have serious consequences. In order to avoid them, keep yourself up to date with the code of practice for your placement school and any organisational policies on data protection. In addition, remind yourself to slow down and be particularly careful whenever you are handling sensitive personal information.

Countersigning

During school placements, teachers may delegate some record keeping to you so that you can develop your ability to monitor and record pupils' progress. A qualified teacher should monitor your work in this area and ensure that any records which you produce, which might be seen by others, are accurate and in keeping with school policy as well as the General Data Protection Regulation (GDPR). For any communications to parents and outside agencies, it is especially important that the records you produce are countersigned by a full-time member of staff before dissemination.

A model for remembering the principles behind good record keeping

While the Teachers' Standards do not provide detailed guidance on record keeping, there are some key principles which schools tend to follow. The following keyword models may help you to keep these principles in mind:

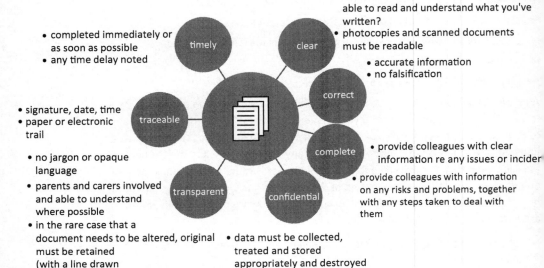

- write with a reader in mind – will they be able to read and understand what you've written?
- photocopies and scanned documents must be readable
- accurate information
- no falsification

- completed immediately or as soon as possible
- any time delay noted

- signature, date, time
- paper or electronic trail

- no jargon or opaque language
- parents and carers involved and able to understand where possible
- in the rare case that a document needs to be altered, original must be retained (with a line drawn through), and new entry should be signed, timed and dated

- provide colleagues with clear information re any issues or incider

- provide colleagues with information on any risks and problems, together with any steps taken to deal with them

- data must be collected, treated and stored appropriately and destroyed following local policy
- be aware of legislation regarding these matters such as GDPR

Figure 2.1: Principles of record keeping

Writing official reports

A report requires you to present and analyse information, and sometimes to provide recommendations. In some ways, report writing is similar to essay writing in that it requires a high degree of planning based on a clear understanding of the following.

- Why are you writing the report? (purpose)
- Who will be reading it? (audience)

This second question can be slightly difficult in report writing. An academic essay usually has only one type of reader, ie a university lecturer. However, a report could potentially have one or several types of reader, eg professionals and the general public. When planning and writing a report, it is very important to bear in mind all the potential readers. Sometimes, two reports are written, one for a professional audience and one for the general public. This is very common in educational research. In addition, if a report is particularly long, a shorter version of the report, called an 'executive summary', tends to accompany the longer report. This allows busy professionals (or, indeed, the general public) to get the gist of the main aspects of the report without having to read all of it.

As well as good planning, a report requires a process of careful drafting and editing, just like an academic essay.

A report must have a clear objective and a very precise structure. When writing a report, first check if there is a standard template that you are expected to adopt. This might include details such as:

- specific headings;
- whether sections should be numbered;
- requirements for a glossary (a list of definitions of key terms).

If there is no template, format the report logically so that it is consistent and easy to navigate.

During their normal working lives, every qualified teacher will have to write a report of some sort. These might include:

- reports related to health and safety issues, such as a risk assessment prior to an educational visit for pupils;
- reports related to a case conference for a pupil with learning or behavioural difficulties;
- reports to parents on their children's progress;
- a report on their analysis of work across the school in a particular subject – for example, if the teacher is subject co-ordinator for mathematics, the report might be based on teaching observations, surveys of children's work and of teachers' planning and marking.

Task

Familiarising yourself with some official reports from professional bodies such as Ofsted can help you to understand the typical format and style of official reports in education. Below are some extracts from an Ofsted report: *Knife Crime: Safeguarding Children and Young People in Education* (2019).

1) Read the extracts quickly (ignoring the gaps for now) just to get the main idea and decide which part of the report they come from by matching them to different sections of the report:

   - Recommendations;
   - Introduction;
   - Executive summary.

A

This report summarises our findings and recommendations from a research project in London on knife crime in education. The research was _____ in 29 schools, colleges and pupil referral units in London and included focus groups with parents and children. We have condensed our findings into recommendations that focus on six areas of practice and policy that need further consideration from central government, local government and school leaders. No single agency, including schools, can _____ on its own. But there are some areas of focus for schools and wider agencies individually, and together, that can be tightened to keep children and young people safer. The areas for consideration include:

- improving partnership working and strategic planning in London;
- sharing and promoting good practice in relation to exclusions and managed moves;
- co-ordinating early _____;
- improving information-sharing;
- teaching the curriculum and supporting children to achieve.

B

Agencies and political leaders across London want to do more to _____ children from knife crime and they are _____. Many are acting independently or in partnership to do the right thing, but it is difficult, not least because London's leaders are each managing competing (_____) priorities, each acting largely with autonomy but within rules set out in statutory guidance.

C

Local community safety partnerships should fully _____ schools, colleges and PRUs in developing and implementing local _____ that aim to address _____ crime and serious youth violence.

2) Now read more carefully and complete the extracts using the words and phrases listed below:

> involve   knife   protect   searching for answers   strategies
> solve knife crime   and sometimes conflicting
> help and prevention   carried out

3) Read the whole report here:
   www.gov.uk/government/publications/knife-crime-safeguarding-children-and-young-people-in-education.
   Do you find it easy to read? Why is this?

4) What do you notice about the way it is written and presented? Consider:

- how it is formatted – the page layout, headings, the use of bullet points, etc;
- the length and content of paragraphs;
- the style and language used.

Top tips

Report writing

1) Bear in mind the **purpose** of the report and keep the prospective **reader** at the forefront of your mind while writing. Ask yourself if they will be able to navigate the report easily, extract the main message, and understand any important details.

2) The purpose of the report and the needs of the reader should determine all **formatting** choices.
   - Is the layout reader-friendly? Does it allow the reader to navigate sections easily?
   - Is the font and use of colour, bold, etc conducive to easy reading?
   - Are the headings meaningful? Do they relate exactly to the content beneath them? Could they be shorter and simpler?
   - Could bullet points help the reader to read a list more easily?

3) You want the reader to take the content seriously so presentation should be to professional standard.

4) Think about how figures and tables may help you to convey your message more clearly.

5) Sentences and paragraphs should be kept quite short wherever possible, and each paragraph should stick to one main idea, preferably indicated in the first sentence.

6) Language should be fairly formal and kept simple wherever possible. Check spelling, grammar and punctuation carefully; again, this is important if the report is to appear serious and professional to the reader.

7) Use colons and semi-colons to present lists, eg:

Respondents identified several areas of concern:

- funding;
- staffing;
- safety.

Task

Improve the report extract below by correcting mistakes in spelling, grammar and punctuation.

Recommendation

Phonics has become a key consideration in teaching of reading, and greater emphasis is now placed on phonic approach and there affectiveness in teaching children to read. There will a reveiw of the phonics approaches in this sceme, in order bring the texts in line with current researches.

CROSS REFERENCE

Academic Writing and Referencing for your Education Degree: Chapter 4, Language in use, Grammar, spelling and punctuation

CROSS REFERENCE

Record keeping

Writing official letters

Teachers often have to write official letters or emails to parents, other education professionals (eg pupil referral units, educational psychologists) or to government agencies. When writing official letters, especially letters to parents, academics and practitioners in education advocate a 'plain English' approach, avoiding Latin terms, educational jargon, and obscure or confusing acronyms and abbreviations. They also stress the importance of transparency and inclusivity, and avoidance of stigmatising language.

Task

Read the example letter from a teacher to a parent and answer the questions.

1) Which address is that of a) the sender and b) the recipient?

2) What does 're' (first line of the letter) mean?

3) The letter starts with 'Dear Mrs Parent' and ends with 'Yours sincerely'. When would you end a letter with 'Yours faithfully'?

4) What is the purpose of the letter?

5) Who will read the letter?

6) Is the language used in the letter suitable for all readers?

7) Does the letter conform to the guidelines on good practice discussed in previous sections of this chapter?

> Woodside School
> Wood Lane
> Ambridge
> AM19 4RR
> 27 April 2019

Mrs A Parent
17 Tree Close
Darrington
AM10 9PP

Dear Mrs Parent,

Re: Sanctions on James Parent

Following your call to the headteacher, Mrs Boss, yesterday, I would like to explain the situation concerning the sanctions which have been placed on James as a result of his behaviour and attitude on the school Easter holiday trip to Whitby.

You stated in your call that you felt James had been unfairly picked on, and that he was just high-spirited. However, while James is undoubtedly a high-spirited boy, he is also old enough and intelligent enough to understand that rules are there for the safety and well-being of all, and to appreciate the effect his behaviour may have on younger children. We feel that James may not have been entirely candid with you about the reasons for his current situation, and so I am writing to make sure you have the full picture. A copy of this letter will also be given to the headteacher, and will go into James' file here at school.

On the coach journey to Whitby, James was clearly excited about the trip, though this does not excuse the way in which he constantly interrupted or talked over the driver's commentary on points of interest. When an adult in charge is talking, it is important that all should pay attention as there may be important safety information.

On the first night at the hostel, my colleague, Mr Chips, discovered all the boys in James' bedroom out of bed and sharing sweets, biscuits and cola drinks at 11.15 pm. All the boys in this incident admitted to having brought 'supplies for the feast' with them, but all independently said that it had been James' idea. Not only were my colleagues and I disturbed, but children in the neighbouring rooms were woken late at night, when they had a busy and active day to come. The boys were spoken to severely in the morning and made to clear up the mess they had made in their room.

Nevertheless, James continued to initiate disruptive behaviour throughout the four days of the stay: this included the organising of downstairs races on the plastic trays provided for storage in the bedrooms, 'ghost visits' to frighten the younger children in their rooms, deciding to go for a walk on the beach before breakfast (despite the inclemency of the prevailing weather) without telling anyone else or asking for permission, and a fight over the washing-up in the kitchen which began with flicked soapsuds and ended with three children in tears, a soaked floor and clothing, and two broken plates. On the beach walks, he spent a lot of time splashing other children with sea water or kicking sand at them when he should have been looking for specimens, and at mealtimes, he either complained loudly and rudely about the food, or pushed other children aside to obtain extra helpings.

In view of this cumulative record, we have asked James to write letters of apology for his behaviour to the manager of the hostel, to the curator of Fenwick Park Museum, whose interesting and valuable talk on Captain Cook was so lamentably interrupted, and to the coach driver, Mr Miles Driver, from Premier Travel. We do not feel this is unreasonable, and as we wish to see these letters before they are mailed, we are keeping James in during the lunchtime break this week so that they can be written under staff supervision. It is important for the good name of the school that this gesture is made, and we feel sure you will support us in this.

James is an intelligent and imaginative boy who should be starting to think not only of his own image and reputation, but also of his future and his school record. We hope that this temporary loss of his recreation time, and the task of writing the letters, will bring this home to him, and we are confident that you, like us, want only to see him achieve his full potential.

If you have any questions about the situation, please contact me at school on 01482 331646 or email ateacher@wssch.co.uk.

Yours sincerely
Ann Teacher
Year 9 Leader
cc. Mrs Boss, Headteacher

Top tips

Using the right salutation and sign-off in official letters and emails

There are two ways to start an official letter, and two ways to end it. The conventions governing the choice of salutation and sign off can seem a little old-fashioned and rather arbitrary, but it is worth knowing about them. In short, if you know the name of the person you are writing to, start with 'Dear Mr _____' or 'Dear Ms/Miss/Mrs _____' and end with 'Yours sincerely'; if you do not know the name of the recipient, start with 'Dear Sir' or 'Dear Madam' and end with 'Yours faithfully'.

OPENING	CLOSING
Dear Mr Brown Dear Ms Gonzalez Dear Mrs Chowdry	Yours sincerely
Dear Sir Dear Madam Dear Sir or Madam	Yours faithfully

A good way to remember this is by noting that you don't use two 's' words ('sir' and 'sincerely') together. With regard to the use of Ms/Miss/Mrs, it is common practice today to use the generic form 'Ms'. However, if you are writing to someone who you know prefers 'Miss' or 'Mrs', then you should probably go with their preference.

Writing information leaflets for parents and carers

Teachers often produce information leaflets for parents. These might focus on a particular aspect of children's learning and provide advice on how parents can support their children in line with the school's approach. Typical examples in primary schools might be a leaflet on helping children with spelling or on supporting children's reading.

As with all the writing discussed in this chapter, to write information leaflets, you need to have a clear idea of the **purpose** of the leaflet, and the needs and expectations of the target **reader** (as well as parents and carers, the leaflet might be read by other family members such as grandparents or older siblings).

A good place to start is to make a list of the kind of questions which a parent or carer might have about the subject. For a leaflet on supporting children's reading these might include:

- What do I do when my child cannot read a word?
- How do I use phonics to help her or him?
- Should I read to my child every day?
- What kinds of texts should I use?

Once you have listed your questions, you need to find authoritative and reliable information to help you to provide helpful answers – Ofsted, websites such as the United Kingdom Literacy Association (UKLA) and some of the resources and textbooks you used when training can be useful sources. You then need to consider how you can make this information accessible to people with no expert knowledge.

It is important that information leaflets are not over-technical, too impersonal or too formal. Readers need to feel comfortable reading the leaflet. It should not be intimidating to readers, but neither should it talk down to them.

Top tips

Writing information leaflets

1) The tone should be conversational – imagine explaining something face to face. Use personal pronouns ('You might want to consider a visit to your local library') and avoid impersonal passive sentences ('Visits to your local library are considered beneficial').

2) The language should be simple and readable. This might mean using short sentences where possible and explaining any difficult or technical words in plain English (digraphs – two letters that make one sound, eg 'ch' in 'chips', 'sh' in 'shop', 'ai' in 'rain').

3) The writing should be concise – avoid any words or phrases which are unnecessary, so that the reader can extract the main message easily.

4) Choose your words carefully – you may use terms such as 'blending' and 'segmenting' on a daily basis with colleagues when discussing phonics, but these words may have different connotations for people who do not work in schools.

Summary

This chapter has explored the different kinds of writing expected of you as a professional teacher. It has looked at how to write records, reports, correspondence and information leaflets, with a focus on achieving your aim, bearing the reader in mind, and writing in a clear, appropriate and effective manner.

References

Baron, B (2018) A Brief History of Singular 'They'. OED blog [online]. Available at: https://public.oed.com/blog/a-brief-history-of-singular-they/ (accessed 19 June 2019).

Department for Education (2011) Teachers' Standards [online]. Available at: www.gov.uk/government/uploads/system/uploads/attachment_data/file/665520/Teachers__Standards.pdf (accessed 26 February 2019).

Hickman, R (2013) *CHEAT: Cambridge Handbook of Educational Abbreviations and Terms*. Cambridge: University of Cambridge Faculty of Education.

Ofsted (2019) *Knife Crime: Safeguarding Children and Young People in Education*. London: Ofsted [online]. Available at: www.gov.uk/government/publications/knife-crime-safeguarding-children-and-young-people-in-education (accessed 27 March 2019).

Chapter 3
Academic presentations and
public speaking

Learning outcomes

After reading this chapter you will:

- be able to approach public speaking with greater confidence;

- be better able to select suitable content for academic presentations and organise it effectively;

- be better able to produce visual aids which support and enhance your academic presentations;

- have developed strategies to enable you to deliver effective academic presentations on the day;

- have an idea of the different types of presentation you might be asked to do at university (individual, group, poster).

Public speaking forms an important part of academic and professional life, and can also feature more widely in our personal lives.

Reflection

1) Have you done any of the following:
   - given an academic presentation?
   - spoken at a political meeting or community event?
   - given a commercial presentation?
   - spoken on TV or radio?
   - spoken on social media, eg in a podcast or a video?
   - done any of the above in a second language?
2) How did you feel about doing these things?
3) How did you prepare?

Oracy skills in academic study

The skill of **public speaking** is an example of what are sometimes referred to as 'oracy skills', ie skills that involve speaking and listening, as opposed to 'literacy skills', which involve reading and writing. There is growing interest in the role of oracy skills in education (see Mercer et al, 2017), and they will undoubtedly form an important part of your degree programme, as well as your future professional life.

For you, as an undergraduate student teacher, the oracy skills that you will develop and be assessed on at university will probably include giving academic **presentations**, both individually and in groups, and participating in group **seminars**. The nature and function of the oracy skills you employ in these different contexts will vary. In a presentation, you will be aiming to present ideas that you have worked through, crafted and refined. In contrast, in a group seminar, you may be trying to express ideas that you are still getting to grips with, testing them to see if they hold water, perhaps adapting them as you listen to what others have to say. So oracy skills are not only a way of demonstrating what you have learned; they are also a learning tool, a way of helping you to process knowledge and work through ideas. They are thus an essential part of critical thinking.

CROSS REFERENCE

Critical Thinking Skills for your Education Degree

This chapter will help you to understand the principles behind public speaking, in particular, academic presentations, and it will provide strategies that you can adapt to your own circumstances and learning preferences. The next chapter will help you to participate more successfully in seminars.

CROSS REFERENCE

Chapter 4, Participating in group seminars and meetings

The following **case studies** demonstrate how people's experience of public speaking and academic presentations differs. The issues they raise will be discussed subsequently in this chapter.

Case studies

Look at the student comments below. Do any of them reflect your own experiences and feelings about public speaking and presentations?

1) 'I quite enjoy speaking in front of an audience.'

2) 'I much prefer giving presentations to writing!'

3) 'I feel sick for a week before I give a presentation.'

4) 'I have butterflies for the first five minutes of a presentation, then I usually relax and enjoy it.'

5) 'English is not my first language so I find it really difficult to present in English and I worry about making mistakes with grammar and pronunciation.'

6) 'I dread questions from the audience – they always throw me.'

7) 'The lecturers on the course ask us to use PowerPoint but I worry that I don't know how to use it as well as other students on my course.'

Giving effective academic presentations

Students arrive at university with varying degrees of experience of academic presentations.

Reflection

1) What experience do you have of:
   - giving academic presentations in front of fellow students, teachers or lecturers?
   - presenting academic papers at conferences?
   - listening to academic presentations?
2) In your opinion, what makes:
   - a good presentation?
   - a bad presentation?

There is no one answer to the question of what makes a good presentation, but the following section provides:

- strategies, advice and tips which can help you prepare an academic presentation and deliver it effectively on the day;
- opportunities for reflection so that you can work out what might work best for you;
- tasks to help you start putting some of what you learn into practice.

Presenting style

There is no single style which defines a good presentation. For example, some people are very animated and entertaining while others are quieter and rather business-like. Both styles, as well as other ways of presenting, can be effective.

Reflection

1) Think back to any time you have been in the audience at a talk, speech or presentation. What kind of presenting styles did you notice? Which did you find most effective?
2) How would you describe your own style of presenting? Has it changed at all with any experience you've gained?

Whatever your personal style, the audience, and your assessors, are generally looking for a presentation which is:

- professional and well prepared;
- clear and easy to follow;
- engaging and interesting.

To ensure that your presentation has these qualities, you need to do a lot of work beforehand. When you see a presentation go smoothly, it is easy to forget the intense effort that has usually gone into making this happen – just as an elegant swan might appear to be gliding effortlessly across the water while their feet are working furiously beneath the surface.

The following sections will elaborate on the things that you can do to prepare your presentation and make sure things go as smoothly as possible on the day. There is also advice on how to cope when things don't go quite as smoothly as you'd hoped (it can happen to us all).

CROSS REFERENCE

Academic Writing and Referencing for your Education Degree, Chapter 1, Academic writing: text, process and criticality

Audience and purpose

When writing, the most important considerations are *your purpose in writing* and *the person reading your text*; likewise, when presenting, the most important considerations are *your purpose in presenting* and *the people listening to you*.

Reflection

1) Discuss the last presentation you gave. What was the purpose of the presentation? Who were the audience?
2) Do you think you achieved what you set out to do?
3) How do you think the audience responded to you?
4) Is there anything you would do differently next time? Why?

If you have ever been in an audience where you felt lost or bored, it could well have been because the presenter misjudged the context of their presentation, and was perhaps thinking more about what *they* wanted to say rather than what *you* wanted or needed to hear. Try to avoid making that same mistake in your own presentations by thinking very carefully about the context of your presentation and preparing it with your **purpose** and a particular **audience** in mind. In your case, you are likely to be presenting to your lecturers and fellow students. This might be in the form of a 'formal' presentation, where you stand at the front of the room and present to an audience seated in front of you, often as part of your assessment. Or it might be a presentation to a group of your peers in a seminar situation, which could also be assessed. Your purpose in the former situation is primarily to demonstrate your knowledge and understanding of the topic. In the latter situation, your purpose could be to set up and lead a group discussion. As you advance in your studies, you may be presenting your research, either to lecturers and fellow students at university, or more widely at conferences. In all cases, the most important thing is to adapt to the context, whatever it is, and to cater for the needs and expectations of the people who will be sitting in front of you.

CROSS REFERENCE

Chapter 4, Participating in group seminars and meetings

Research and preparation

Preparation, involving research and the selection, organisation and presentation of information and ideas, is essential to a good presentation.

Reflection

1) What factors do you consider when selecting content for a presentation?

2) What do you aim to achieve when organising your content? What do you think are the principles of good organisation?

3) Do you ever go over time when giving presentations? If so, why do you think this is?

CROSS REFERENCE

Appendix 1, Academic levels at university

It is important that you research the topic carefully and, particularly at levels 5 and 6, *critically*. Your lecturers will be looking for you to show that you are in full command of the material. This doesn't necessarily mean knowing every last detail about every aspect of the topic. In fact, your lecturers will expect you to be selective and to acknowledge any areas of doubt. This is part of being a *critical* student.

Selecting and processing information and ideas

When researching a topic, you are likely to encounter a great deal of information. It is therefore important that you establish the **scope** of your presentation, based on purpose and audience, **select** material which is appropriate, relevant and, hopefully, interesting for your audience, and then **process** that material so that your audience will be able to digest it easily. When selecting which material you will choose to cover and how much detail you will go into, it is important to consider the following questions.

- How much is your audience likely to know about the topic? It's important that you **pitch your presentation at the right level**. You don't want to talk down to people in the room, but neither do you want what you say to go completely over people's heads. Consider which concepts and terminology you can assume knowledge of, and which you may need to define and explain. Remember, if the concept or terminology was new to *you*, then it's likely that you will need to explain it to other students at the same level. And even though your lecturers are very likely to already know about the concepts and terminology in your presentation, they will be expecting you to explain a great deal in order to demonstrate your own knowledge and understanding. And remember, even lecturers don't know everything! They often learn something new from student presentations and are very happy to do so.

- How can you **make the topic accessible** to your audience? Some aspects of the topics you present may well be complex and difficult to understand. Think about how you can help the audience to process information, perhaps by breaking things down or explaining things in a step-by-step fashion. You may also be able to support your explanations with diagrams, or use vivid examples to clarify a point.

- How can you **make the topic interesting** for your audience? Have you ever listened to a presentation where the presenter seemed intent on telling you every last detail of a topic without regard for what you, the audience, might want or need to know? This is often a sign that presenters have not considered the audience at the planning stage. They could be very competent presenters, but if they have only thought about *what they want to say*, rather than *what this particular audience might want or need to hear*, they will find it hard to engage the audience. Effective presenters, on the other hand, think about what is appropriate and relevant for the people in front of them and then think about how they can convey these things in the most accessible, interesting way possible.

- How can you **say what you have to say in the time available**? Practise giving your presentation several times, and time yourself to make sure that the content you have selected fits the time you have been allotted. Be careful when adding or deleting content as this can affect the coherence of your presentation. One easy way to extend or shorten a presentation can be to add or delete discrete examples, as these can be easy to slot in or take out without affecting the general flow of information and ideas. Remember, it is unprofessional to go over time, and, in assessments, or at conferences, you may be cut off before the end of your talk if you do so. In assessments, you may also be penalised.

Top tips

Telling a story

Some of the most effective and interesting presentations involve a 'story'. This could be an account of how an area of knowledge has evolved, or it could even be the story of your own research into the topic – how your knowledge and understanding developed as you surveyed the literature, and what interested or surprised you most along the way.

Organising information and ideas

Once you have selected information to be included, you need to **organise** it in the most effective manner.

- **Make it flow.** You need to structure your content in a clear, logical manner, so that it flows and is easy to follow. This will probably entail experimenting with different ways of organising what you want to say. You might find it useful to use a mind map, or to write headings and sub-headings on cards and then physically move them around.

- **Keep it simple.** Break down long segments of information into 'manageable chunks', especially if they are dense and complex. Use simple two/three/four-part organisational structures where possible. Complex content benefits from a simple organisation structure. What's more, the simpler the organisation, the easier it is for you to remember what comes next when you are delivering your presentation.

Task

What simple organisational structures could you use to structure presentations on the following topics?

1) The teaching family in schools in the twenty-first century.

2) The role of teaching assistants and higher level teaching assistants.

3) Supporting children with learning difficulties.

Visual aids

Any visual aids such as PowerPoint slides should be of a professional standard and should be there primarily to help the audience to follow your talk, rather than simply entertaining them or, worse, bombarding them with information.

Reflection

1) What features of PowerPoint do you tend to use (think about design, colour, animations, transitions, etc)? Why do you use these features in the way you do?

2) Have you used other presentation software such as Prezi? What are the advantages and disadvantages of alternatives to PowerPoint?

The following guidelines should help you to produce slides which are an effective enhancement to your words.

Font

- Choose a font size that's visible at the back of a large room (24 pt is usually the lower limit, but it depends on the other factors – room, size of screen, etc).

- Be wary of using **bold**, *italics*, underlining or CAPITALISATION to convey subtleties of meaning as these can be hard to read on screen, especially for anyone who is dyslexic.

Colour

- Make sure there is a clear colour contrast between background and text (and remember that just because things look clear on your computer at home, it doesn't mean they will necessarily be clear on a classroom screen with different resolution and lighting conditions – always check *in situ*).

- Avoid using red and green together, as people who have a colour vision deficiency (the formal name for 'colour blindness') cannot distinguish between them.

Effects

- Avoid decorative background images that may obscure the text.
- Choose animations and transitions which are simple and effective, rather than just being there to decorate your slides or entertain.
- Be careful with moving images or flashing effects as they may be distracting or irritating – they may also be dangerous for people with epilepsy or light sensitivity.
- Make good use of the 'appear' function in PowerPoint, and practise synchronising this with your speaking: if you incorporate this feature into your slides, but then introduce all your bullet points randomly or all at once, it rather defeats the object!
- Limit the number of slides, and make sure that you are not moving through slides too quickly.

Text and images

- Make sure your slides are not cluttered with text and images.
- Limit the amount of text on the slides to 'manageable chunks', which are easily digestible.
- The text on your slides should be mostly limited to **brief prompts** (rather than full sentences) which you expand on as you speak. On slides, you can sometimes leave out 'grammar' words like verbs or words like 'a' or 'the' in a way that would not be acceptable in an essay. This is because the text on PowerPoint slides can function as a kind of shorthand. However, be careful with this if English is not your first language – it can be difficult for non-native speakers of a language to judge which grammatical words are necessary or not. If in doubt, retain the words in question.
- Do not read text verbatim from your slides. (You will bore your audience rigid and audience members are capable of reading what's on the slides!)
- Make sure that every word, diagram and label is clearly visible, even from the back of the room. Also, make sure you have referenced those images taken from sources. (See the example slides on the following pages for examples of **Creative Commons** images, which can often be freely used without the need for acknowledgement.)
- Proofread your slides carefully to check for accuracy and consistency of formatting.

Training

- Universities often provide training on the use of PowerPoint. Check your library website for courses.

Task

Look at the following presentation slides and answer the questions.
(The notes provided after each slide provide some possible answers.)

1) How has the student used the slides to organise the presentation?

2) Are the slides clear and easy to read?

3) How has the student used diagrams to support and enhance the presentation?

The teaching 'family' in schools

A summative presentation by
Charlotte Coppinger, First-Year Educational Studies

20 May 2019

The title slide should include the title of the presentation, together with the name of the presenter, date and occasion for which it is presented.

The British Dyslexia Association provides a dyslexia-friendly style guide aimed to help people design their handouts and PowerPoint presentations in a dyslexia-friendly manner. They suggest avoiding white backgrounds on paper or online, including visual aids, as white can appear too dazzling, and suggest using cream or a soft pastel colour. Some dyslexic people will have their own colour preference. Fonts should be plain, evenly spaced sans serif fonts such as Arial. Alternatives include Verdana, Tahoma, Century Gothic and Trebuchet.

Aims of the presentation

During this presentation, we will:

- explore the different types of workers within the teaching family;
- discuss what a 'teacher' is;
- explore skills involved in teaching;
- debate whether skill mix and the teaching family are good for teachers and for teaching.

It is good practice to identify some aims for your presentation. Slides generally should not be too cluttered. Any pictures or diagrams should not encroach on the copy (text) area and you should check out any copyright issues. Creative Commons images (see http://creativecommons.org) can be used freely or with simple acknowledgments. The 'bulls eye' image in the slide above is a Creative Commons 'CC0' image, which means there are no restrictions on its use, nor is any acknowledgement required.

Teaching

Different people teach in schools:

- teaching assistants (TAs);
- higher level teaching assistants (HLTAs);
- student teachers;
- supply teachers;
- peripatetic teachers;
- unqualified teachers;
- qualified teachers.

Pictures can help. The image here, like all of the images in this presentation, is also a CC0 image, so it does not need any attribution.

Qualified Teacher Status (QTS)

- Traditionally, most teachers have had QTS.
- Unqualified teachers have always been allowed to teach in private schools.
- Unqualified teachers can now also teach in academies and free schools.

With bulleted lists, you might want to use some of the 'animation' options in PowerPoint to introduce each bullet in turn.

Different routes into teaching

There are now several different ways to achieve QTS:

- undergraduate or PGCE course at a university;
- School Direct;
- School Centred Initial Teacher Training (SCITT);
- Teach First;
- Troops into Teaching.

Simple images and a small amount of text work well in slides. Don't go overboard with text – some might even argue there is too much text in this slide.

Dumbing down?

- Pupils and parents don't necessarily know if the person teaching has QTS.
- TAs and HLTAs can teach classes.
- Does the limited training of some 'teachers' put pupils at risk?
- Would unqualified people be allowed in other professions? Doctors? Dentists? Pilots?

DUMBING DOWN

meaning, definition, explanation...

It can be useful to have discrete slides for the different sides of the argument you might be presenting.

Counter-arguments

- There is currently a teacher shortage – we need more teachers, even if not all have received lengthy training.
- Not everyone needs lengthy training.
- TAs and HLTAs can release teachers to focus on children's needs.
- TAs and HLTAs can work under guidance of teachers.

This is another example of a discrete slide for another side of an argument.

Conclusion

- Not everyone who teaches has a teaching qualification.
- High levels of skill and knowledge are needed to teach.
- The broader 'teaching family' can strengthen or dilute teaching, depending on your perspective.

It's always good to have a summing up slide with a few 'headline' statements.

Presentation aims (revisited)

During this presentation, we have:
- explored the different types of workers within the teaching family;
- discussed what a 'teacher' is;
- explored skills involved in teaching;
- debated whether skill mix and the teaching family are good for teachers and for teaching.

Towards the end of your presentation, you might want to revisit your aims and check with the audience that you have covered them.

THANK YOU FOR LISTENING

QUESTIONS?

The final slide often has a 'thank you' on it and, if appropriate, a call for questions.

On the day

As mentioned previously in the chapter, successful presentations can be delivered in a range of individual styles. As also mentioned, a lot of what happens on the day is down to your prior research and preparation, and a good understanding of context, purpose and audience. It is then a case of doing all you can to make sure that you deliver your presentation effectively on the day.

Reflection

1) How do you prepare yourself for a presentation?
2) Do you do anything to control nerves or anxiety?
3) Do you use notes during presentations? If so, how do you use them?

There are a number of useful strategies that you can adopt during your presentation to engage the audience, control nerves and make things go as smoothly as possible.

- If you are nervous before your presentation, it may help to slow your breathing or drink some water. It is OK to have water available to sip during your presentation too.

- During the presentation, address the audience directly, rather than facing the screen to read from slides or continually lowering your head to read notes. Think of a presentation as a two-way process, a conversation with the audience rather than a performance. If you engage the audience, they will communicate with you in a way through their body language, as well as through questions at the end of your presentation.

- Make eye contact with the audience, almost as you would in a conversation with someone, taking care to include as much of the room as possible. In an assessment situation, the assessors do not want you to focus on them – in fact, they will be taking note of how you establish rapport with the whole audience, how you endeavour to engage the whole room.

- Project your voice so that everyone in the room can hear you.

- Vary your intonation and pace, foregrounding and backgrounding information as required, slowing down to make something clear or to focus on a particular point; try to avoid speaking in a flat, monotone voice.

- Don't speak too quickly. It's quite common for people to speak too quickly in presentations, especially if they are nervous. Some presenters may also speak quickly to fit everything in, usually because they have not been disciplined in their selection of content. Remember also, if English is your second language, speed does not equal fluency in a language. Listen to experienced presenters and you will notice that they tend to slow down their speech on long words or when a word has particular importance. Try to do this yourself.

- Adopt a physical stance which feels relaxed and comfortable. This usually means moving around a little bit rather than standing in one place, and using your arms and hands as a natural part of communication. For example, you will probably want to physically indicate certain information on your slides at certain points.

- If you use notes, use them in a smart way. It is impressive if you can speak confidently and naturally without notes. However, many people prefer to have some notes at hand as an *aide memoire*, often written on small cards – or in the notes section of PowerPoint – just in case they get lost or forget something. This is fine – it is a good strategy to have. Just make sure you manage to look up at the audience most of the time. It is of course not a good thing to read verbatim from notes as if from an essay, or from your slides – this is extremely boring for the audience.

- Don't panic. If you lose your train of thought, pause and consult your notes or slides. Audiences are usually fairly sympathetic – they probably know how you feel.

- Practise several times to help you remember what you want to say, refine your delivery and increase your confidence. But don't learn by rote: it will sound unnatural if you try to recite something you have memorised, and straining to remember every word will make you stressed and preoccupied during the actual presentation, preventing engagement with the audience. Each practice should follow the same basic structure but there should also be some natural variation.

Top tips

Speaking well

- **Accuracy** is important, but, if English is not your first language, do not worry about making a few mistakes, as long as these do not interfere with **communication**.

- You should aim for a reasonably formal **style** – you shouldn't be too 'chatty' or vague, and you should always avoid slang.

- **Pronunciation** and **articulation** are very important. The most important thing is to be clear, and slowing down to clearly articulate key terms can help achieve this. Check the pronunciation of **key words** beforehand. Use an online dictionary with sound function (or a specialised reference work for very technical words), especially if English is not your first language. Assessors will not penalise you for having an accent (we all do!) or for the occasional mispronunciation, but they will be irritated if you keep mispronouncing a key word, and they will be unable to follow you if they cannot make out which word you are trying to say. Preparing the language you are going to use can also help you feel more in control and thus help reduce anxiety.

Top tips

Starting well!

- Greet the audience and introduce yourself, but keep it short and to the point:

  'Good morning/afternoon, my name is Gong Yi and I'm going to talk about…'

  'I am Jane Berk, from the University of Glasgow, and my main area of research is…'

- Make sure that the main subject of your talk is clearly pronounced/articulated and that it is written on the first slide.

- Try to arouse the interest of your audience with an interesting fact/anecdote/question, etc.

- Provide a clear outline of how your talk will progress – but, again, make it concise

Ending well

- This is a chance to re-state the **main message** of your presentation in a concise, effective way. Keep it short and sweet! Be careful not to start repeating yourself in an unstructured manner.

- End the presentation cleanly and decisively – try not to waffle or repeat yourself:

  'So that concludes my presentation. Thank you. Does anyone have any questions?'

Top tips

Dealing with questions

- Try to predict the most likely questions and prepare for them.

- Be prepared to reformulate questions to make sure you have understood, and to make sure the audience have also heard and understood.

- Go back to the relevant slide if necessary.

- Never have anything on your slides that you cannot explain – someone may ask you about it!

Group presentations

Group presentations present particular opportunities and challenges. They are an example of collaborative learning, something which is highly valued in universities, and many students benefit greatly from working so closely with fellow students. However, working as a group can also bring difficulties, and you will need to be prepared to address issues as they arise. Ultimately, working in a group is a learning experience in itself and you should take the opportunity to reflect on how you felt during the process and what this means for your future development (see Cartney and Rouse, 2006).

CROSS REFERENCE

Studying for your Education Degree, Chapter 2, Strategies for effective learning, Collaboration in action

Top tips

Working in groups

1) Agree on some basic ground rules at the beginning of the process.

2) Establish good channels of communication, either face to face or online.

3) Conduct all communication with respect and sensitivity.

4) Make the group as inclusive as possible by informing and involving everyone, and by recognising individual strengths and contributions.

5) Create an agenda for each meeting, preferably sent out beforehand so that people can prepare. During the meeting, ask for a volunteer to make notes alongside each point. You can then put these online so that everyone is clear about what has been agreed and who is responsible for any action points.

6) Encourage a constructive atmosphere where people listen to each other and acknowledge each other, negotiating respectfully and building on others' points. Give some thought to the physical arrangement of the room – is it conducive to good communication?

Poster presentations

Poster presentations are an alternative to oral presentations with slides. They are a common feature of conferences, where they can be used to present research findings, make people aware of a shared resource, or invite collaboration. For university students, they are sometimes used as a form of assessment. A student, or a group of students, will be required to create a poster which presents a summary of their research into a given topic. As with all presentations, and just as with academic writing, the purpose and audience should determine the scope and depth of the content.

Posters can be created manually, but they are usually created with bespoke software packages. These will usually be available through your library or IT website, and you may also be able to get some training on using these packages. Posters are created using both text and images (figures, graphs, tables, etc), and there are usually facilities available on campus where you can have your poster published to a professional standard, usually for a small fee.

Posters are presented in a public forum. This often resembles a type of 'market place', with people stopping to read the posters and comment or ask questions, before moving on to the next 'stall'. In this case, the poster should encourage people to engage in a dialogue about your work – though remember to also give them time to read. Alternatively, posters may stand alone without commentary. You need to consider the format of the presentation carefully when you are designing the poster, as it may well help determine the degree of explicitness required.

Posters should, above all, be clear and coherent. They should be easy to navigate, so that people can extract and process information easily. However, they also present an opportunity for you to distil complex information in a creative way.

Top tips

Creating effective posters

- Choose a title that will attract people to your poster. Short, snappy titles can be effective, as can questions (which are answered by the poster).

- Use a clear, layout, with distinct sections, headings and sub-headings. It's usually a good idea to keep things quite simple.

- Have a clear, logical flow of information. Try to imagine how the reader's eye will move over the poster. Think about how you might use features such as panels and arrows to guide them.

- Make sure all the text, including labels for figures and tables, is legible, with a font size (usually no smaller than 24 pt) that can be read at a reasonable distance.

- Keep text to a minimum, avoiding long, dense passages and making good use of concise bullet points.

- Think about how you might use diagrams, graphs and tables to present complex information in an accessible way.

- Have a good balance of text and images, and don't attempt to fill every bit of space.

- Use a limited range of colours so that the poster does not look too busy or garish. Make sure there is a clear contrast between background and text.

Peer review

It is vital to practise your presentation, and this affords an excellent opportunity to incorporate peer review into your practice. Some assessment tasks may also take account of feedback from your peers. When conducting peer reviews in practice sessions, it is a good idea to put together a feedback sheet like the one in Figure 3.1 to use to review each other's presentations, as this will both help you to give useful feedback to your fellow students and encourage you to reflect on how you can improve your own performance.

SPEAKER: TOPIC:	YES/NO	NOTES/ COMMENTS
1) Were you able to follow the general gist of the presentation?		
2) Was the information clearly and logically organised?		
3) Was there an appropriate amount of detail?		
4) Were specialist concepts and terminology adequately defined and explained?		
5) Did the slides help you to understand the topic and follow the line of argument?		
6) Were any words/phrases hard to catch because they were said too quickly or mispronounced?		
7) Did the presenter engage you as an audience member? How? How could they have done this more?		
8) Did the presenter keep to time?		

Figure 3.1: Example peer review sheet

Being assessment literate

Presentations, both individual presentations and group presentations, are a common form of assessment. As with any assessment, it is important to inform yourself of what is required and how you will be assessed. This is sometimes referred to as being '**assessment literate**' (Price et al, 2012). You can become assessment literate by paying close attention to the **wording of the task**, and by familiarising yourself with both the **assessment guidelines** and the **marking descriptors** for the task. Lecturers themselves will refer closely to these when assessing your presentation, so it is very important that you pay close attention to them throughout the planning and practice stages of your presentation.

Below are some example presentation tasks at levels 4, 5 and 6, followed by a table containing marking descriptors which distinguish between what is expected at the three levels (4, 5, 6) of your undergraduate degree.

CROSS
REFERENCE

Appendix 1,
Academic
levels at
university

Example assessment tasks

1) Present to your seminar group a 20-minute presentation on 'daily life in English primary schools' (level 4).

2) In groups of four to five, deliver a 15-minute presentation on 'working with children with English as an additional language' (level 4).

3) In a 20-minute presentation (including question time), answer the question 'Should teachers develop mindfulness in pupils?' (level 5).

4) Deliver a group presentation on the evidence base for allowing HLTAs to teach whole classes on a regular basis. You will have 15 minutes to present and 5 minutes for questions (level 5).

5) In a 20-minute presentation (including question time), critically outline how you would improve classroom management in a classroom in which you have spent time (level 6).

6) 'Unqualified teachers should not be employed as full-time teachers.' Critically explore this statement in a 20-minute presentation with four or five of your peers (level 6).

Table 3.1: Example presentation marking descriptors

Level 4
- Demonstrates knowledge and understanding of the topic area.
- Provides clear slides or other visual prompts that are accessible by all, including those with a disability.
- Demonstrates good verbal and non-verbal communication skills (tone of voice, body language, demeanour, etc).

- Keeps to time and paces the presentation well.
- (For group presentations) Demonstrates reasonable rapport with fellow presenters.

Level 5

- Demonstrates critical understanding of the topic area by providing arguments for and against.
- Provides clear slides or other visual prompts that are accessible by all, including those with a disability.
- Demonstrates good verbal and non-verbal communication skills (tone of voice, body language, demeanour, etc).
- Keeps to time and paces the presentation well.
- Responds to questions posed by the audience confidently.
- (For group presentations) Demonstrates rapport with fellow presenters.
- (For group presentations) Transitions to fellow presenters are good.

Level 6

- Demonstrates critical evaluation of the topic area by making reference to the evidence base.
- Shows emerging evidence of originality in the arguments made.
- Provides clear slides or other visual prompts that are accessible by all, including those with a disability.
- Demonstrates a high level of verbal and non-verbal communication skills (tone of voice, body language, demeanour, etc).
- Keeps to time and paces the presentation well.
- Responds to questions posed by the audience confidently.
- (For group presentations) Clear evidence of rapport with, and seamless transitions between, fellow presenters.

Task

1) Look at the assessment tasks and marking descriptors laid out above. What are the main differences between levels in terms of what is expected from students? What particular phrases in the presentation tasks and marking descriptors tell you this?

2) Brainstorm some ideas for each of the presentation tasks. Which of the tasks seem most interesting to you? Why? Which seem most difficult? Why?

3) Which of the descriptors do you think present the biggest challenges for you as you develop as an academic presenter?

Advanced skills

Three minute thesis

When you are at the stage of writing a dissertation, or even conducting postgraduate research, you will need to present your research to various audiences. When you are deep into a research topic, it can be difficult to shift your perspective to match that of people who have not been on your particular research journey. Many presenters can get bogged down in the detail of their research and ultimately fail to convey the essence of their topic. It could help you to avoid this pitfall if you have a look at some of the entries to the **three minute thesis** competition founded by the University of Queensland (2008). The idea for the competition originated in a slightly unusual way:

'The idea for the 3MT competition came about at a time when the state of Queensland was suffering severe drought. To conserve water, residents were encouraged to time their showers, and many people had a three minute egg timer fixed to the wall in their bathroom. The then Dean of the UQ Graduate School, Emeritus Professor Alan Lawson, put two and two together and the idea for the 3MT competition was born.'

Students entering the competition are required to 'effectively explain their research in three minutes, in a language appropriate to a non-specialist audience', using only one slide. Many universities invite their students to take part in the competition, and most have a web page with videos of some of the best entries. Watching some of these may give you an idea of how to identify the essential components of your research topic and to distil them into something which an audience can easily process and fully appreciate.

Summary

This chapter has explored the nature and challenges of public speaking, with a focus on the types of academic presentation which are likely to be a requirement of your degree programme. It has provided strategies for preparing and delivering presentations, both as an individual and in groups, in an effective, engaging way, focusing on content, organisation, visual aids and delivery. It has also provided examples of tasks at different levels of your degree programmes, along with example descriptors which show what is expected of you at each level.

References

Cartney, P and Rouse, A (2006) The Emotional Impact of Learning in Small Groups: Highlighting the Impact on Student Progression and Retention. *Teaching in Higher Education*, 111(1): 79–81.

Mercer, N, Warwick, P and Ahmed, A (2017) An Oracy Assessment Toolkit: Linking Research and Development in the Assessment of Students' Spoken Language Skills at Age 11–12. *Learning and Instruction*, 48: 51–60.

Price, M, Rust, C, O'Donovan, B and Handley, K (2012) *Assessment Literacy: The Foundation for Improving Student Learning*. Oxford: Oxford Brookes University Press.

Three Minute Thesis, University of Queensland [online]. Available at: https://threeminutethesis.uq.edu.au/home (accessed 28 April 2019).

Chapter 4
Participating in group seminars and meetings

Learning outcomes

After reading this chapter you will:

- be better prepared to participate in group discussion;

- have a good understanding of the role that group discussion and seminars play both in your studies and in your intellectual development;

- be aware of the transferable nature of seminar skills;

- be able to participate more fully and confidently in group discussions, seminars and meetings in academic and professional life;

- have explored strategies to help you participate more effectively in group discussions, seminars and meetings, and to get more from them.

This chapter looks at the topic of group discussion, particularly in the form of seminars. It explores the role seminars play in your university studies, and it familiarises you with certain conventions and language which are important in a seminar setting. This knowledge will help you to participate more fully in seminars. You will also develop an understanding of how the skills you develop in seminars can transfer to your professional life, and help you in teamwork activities and meetings.

The role of seminars at university

Group discussion is an important part of university life, and seminars are the main type of group discussion at university. Seminars usually involve relatively small numbers of students, usually around 8 to 12, but this can vary across institutions and courses. You may or may not have participated in seminars previously, but before reading more about them in this chapter, take some time to reflect on what you think might be the aims and outcomes of seminars.

Task

1) What do you think is the purpose of a seminar?

2) Below are some statements about seminars. Did you think of any of these when answering question 1?

a) Seminars provide an opportunity to follow up on a lecture. They allow you to explore and demonstrate your understanding of the topic, and to clarify anything that you didn't understand from the lecture itself.

b) Seminar discussion can enable you to forge a deeper understanding of ideas and concepts.

c) Seminar discussions can be good preparation for essays, exams and other assessments, as they provide a space for you to test your understanding and ideas, and work out how to express them in a clear, convincing way.

d) Seminars provide an opportunity to learn from people with different knowledge, background, experience and perspectives from your own.

e) Seminar discussion may lead you to change, develop or adapt your opinions and ideas as you come into contact with others' views.

f) Some seminar activities can help you develop your problem-solving skills.

g) Frequent participation in seminars can help you become more confident about public speaking.

h) Seminars can help you become more confident about discussing complex issues and ideas.

i) Seminars can help you improve the way you interact with others in a group setting.

j) Seminar skills are transferable skills which can help you in your professional practice, for example in teamwork and meetings with colleagues.

3) Which of the things mentioned in the statements above do you think are most important for you as a university student?

4) Which of the statements do you think refer to:
- developing your **communication** skills;
- developing your **thinking**;
- both of these?

As the statements in the task explain, seminars can be used to develop or test your understanding of a topic. On some courses they are used as a form of **assessment**, testing both your knowledge of a topic and your ability to interact successfully in a group discussion. Below, there are some examples of typical seminar tasks at different levels, with an indication of how they would be assessed.

CROSS REFERENCE

Appendix 1, Academic levels at university

Example seminar tasks and assessment criteria

Example 1 (level 4)

'You were given a paper to read on the history of education for this week's seminar. Based on your reading of this paper (and any other materials you may have read), together with your direct experience of teaching so far, discuss with your seminar group colleagues the statement "teaching was better in the past than it is now".

If the seminar is assessed, a student's engagement in the seminar might be judged according to the following criteria.

- *Provided evidence that they have read the paper beforehand.*
- *Made a positive contribution to the group.*
- *Provided strong arguments for or against teaching being better in the past than it is now.*
- *Acted in a professional and courteous manner when interacting with others.*

Example 2 (level 5)

'In small groups, spend 10–15 minutes critically exploring the role that teaching assistants can play in:
- integrating pupils with specific learning difficulties into mainstream classes;
- promoting positive attitudes to learning (rather than just supporting pupils with learning difficulties).'

If the seminar is assessed, a student's engagement in the seminar might be judged according to the following criteria.

- *Made a positive contribution to the group.*
- *Provided examples of how teaching assistants might integrate pupils with specific learning difficulties into mainstream classes and promote positive attitudes to learning.*
- *Provided evidence of critical ability (eg challenging others' views, offering alternative stances, referring to the evidence base).*
- *Acted in a professional and courteous manner when interacting with others.*

Example 3 (level 6)

'With your seminar group colleagues, pick one of the three case scenarios that were published to the group last week and provide a plan to support the pupil's development.'

If the seminar is assessed, a student's engagement in the seminar might be judged according to the following criteria.

- *Contributed to the group choice of case scenario.*
- *Provided strong evidence for the use (or not, as the case may be) of a particular teaching model.*
- *Demonstrated critical use of the teaching process (or other problem-solving approach).*
- *Contributed to the evidence base for the plan.*
- *Acted in a professional and courteous manner when interacting with others.*
- *Demonstrated leadership skills (eg actively facilitates discussion, encourages others to speak, actively listens to others).*

The conventions of seminars

Like all community activities, seminars are governed by certain conventions of behaviour. All conventions are determined by the norms, values and practices of the community in question, in this case the academic community. Seminar conventions are intended to facilitate discussion, promote academic activity and development, and help the people involved feel comfortable and engaged.

Reflection

Look at some of the conventions associated with successful seminar participation below:

- preparing before the seminar;
- turn taking;
- making a contribution to the discussion;
- making eye contact with the whole group when you speak;
- backing up your ideas and arguments with clear explanation and reasoning;
- supporting your ideas and arguments with evidence and examples where possible;
- reformulating what you have said if others appear not to understand;
- acknowledging others' contributions and building on them;
- paying attention to others when they are speaking and listening carefully to what they have to say;
- asking for clarification when you haven't understood somebody else's point;
- expressing agreement;
- expressing cautious agreement;
- expressing polite disagreement;
- challenging others' ideas and arguments when you think they are wrong or unclear;
- interrupting politely;
- inviting others to participate;
- reaching a consensus (particularly with problem-solving activities);
- summing up the discussion.

1) Why do you think these things are considered to be important?
2) Can you think of examples which demonstrate their importance?
3) How do they relate to the requirements of the assessments in the previous section to be 'professional' and 'courteous' in interaction with others?
4) Which ones could relate to the 'leadership' requirements of the assessments (facilitating discussion, encouraging others to speak, actively listening to others)?

Task

Look at the extracts from student seminars below. Which of the conventions in the previous reflection task are they related to?

1) 'Wouldn't you say that poverty is a factor here?'

2) 'Yes, but what about parity of opportunity between the private and maintained sectors?'

3) 'But surely that's the role of government?'

4) 'What do you think, Harriet?'

5) 'As Faisal said, the policy seems to disadvantage children from poorer homes and advantage the government, who essentially save money by putting the onus on parents.'

6) 'I think Finland is a good example of somewhere where state education is given a high priority.'

7) 'Did you say you worked with children with dyslexia on your placement, Lia?'

8) 'Could I just add something to what Nerumalia said?'

9) 'Aren't we forgetting the impact of peer pressure?'

10) 'But isn't that more an issue of compliance? Or is it "concordance" or "adherence" that we use now?'

11) 'I take your point, but what about parental involvement?'

12) 'I see what you mean, but why is that important?'

13) 'According to one of the studies we were asked to look at, there is some evidence to suggest that the strategy can be effective if it is combined with other strategies.'

14) 'But didn't that study have a really small sample size?'

15) 'I didn't quite catch what you said about the stats.'

16) 'Sorry, could you just explain what you mean by "alternative strategies"? I ask because lots of different strategies with widely varying evidence bases get lumped together under that heading.'

17) 'I'm afraid I don't quite follow your point.'

18) 'So what you're saying is that we need to provide different types of support.'

19) 'Yes, that's a really good example.'

20) 'Yes, I hadn't thought of that.'

21) "Are you sure about that? It's not how I interpreted it.'

22) 'I don't really think that what you're suggesting is realistic, given the current financial crisis in schools.'

23) "Are we all agreed on that?'

Participating effectively in seminars

n order to participate effectively in seminars, it is important to be aware of the conventions discussed in the previous section, understand why they are important and be willing to adhere to them wherever possible. Some of these conventions will be discussed in more detail in the following sections.

Being prepared

You may be asked to read some material before the seminar, for example, a research article or some case studies. One or two students may be asked to lead the seminar by summarising and commenting on the reading material, leading to a wider group discussion. Preparation could also involve researching different views and perspectives on a topic.

Good preparation should enable you to participate in the seminar. And if you are indeed well prepared, it is a pity to waste all that work by staying silent. If you do not contribute during the seminar, it may signal a lack of preparation or engagement, which will not be appreciated by your lecturers or fellow students, and which could lead to poor marks if you are being assessed.

On the other hand, whereas good preparation is essential, and it is clearly good to have an idea of what you are going to say during the seminar, try not to be too 'rehearsed'. A seminar should promote natural dialogue rather than generate formal speeches.

Top tips

Summarising articles

You can use certain verbs to help you structure your article summary.

1) Giving an overview

The article The author	deals with examines discusses reports on argues that found (that)

2) Indicating the structure of the article

The article The author	begins/starts by _____ing goes on to... then... ends/finishes by _____ing concludes that...

3) Identifying strengths and weaknesses of the article

The article The author	was interesting in that it... puts forward a strong argument in favour of... identifies the probable cause of... did not address... fails to mention... confuses the issue, in my view...

Helping to construct meaning

Seminars are an opportunity to create and explore ideas as a group in a way that would perhaps not be possible on an individual level. Ideally, the ideas discussed are 'emergent and co-constructed', rather than 'presented as already formed for inspection' (Alexander et al, 2011, p 237). People in the group work together to make sense of the issues, ideas, data, etc and are therefore ultimately able to establish better understanding and deeper meaning. You will take your individual thoughts and ideas (and doubts) into the seminar, just as others bring their own thoughts and ideas (and doubts). What is expected is that interaction and collaboration will lead to an interesting synthesis of ideas, and that this will allow individuals to reach conclusions that they could not have reached alone in their room with their lecture notes and books.

Interacting with the group

Successful group interaction is dependent on a number of factors. These are centred around:

- being fully engaged and encouraging others to be fully engaged;
- feeling respected and respecting each other;
- feeling comfortable and making others feel comfortable.

This involves the following.

CROSS REFERENCE

Chapter 1, Professional speaking skills, Active listening

- **Speaking**. It is important that all members of the group make a contribution of some kind. Your individual contribution will vary according to the day or the topic. Sometimes, you may make a significant contribution because you feel confident that you are in full command of the study material or you feel passionate about the topic. Other times, you may make a smaller contribution. This may even just involve responding to another student's contribution, but this in itself can be important. Note that complete silence denotes a lack of involvement and engagement, which is not good for you or for the group. For some people, it can be a bit nerve-wracking to speak for the first time in front of a group, but try to reassure yourself that the second time will almost undoubtedly be easier. Most universities keep students in the same seminar groups for a period of time so that supportive relationships can develop.

- **Listening**. Good listening skills are as important as good speaking skills. The way you respond to someone else's ideas contributes to the general discussion. Your responses are a way of showing that you are fully engaged and paying close attention to what other people are saying. How you respond can also say as much about your intellectual abilities as does your expression of your own ideas, which is particularly important if the seminar task is being assessed.

- **Body language**. There are a number of things which people sometimes do without thinking, and even though the people who do these things may not mean any disrespect, their actions may signal a lack of interest and engagement, or imply that they are not taking the seminar seriously. These include: looking down or away when someone is talking, checking phones, eye rolling, sighing or tutting.

- **Being assertive without being rude**. This can be tricky to navigate, but it is essential to bear it in mind. While it is important to be able to say what you think in a confident way, and to be able to disagree with others when necessary, it is also crucial that you do this without upsetting people or causing the discussion to become strained. Politeness is related to the words you use, the tone of your voice, and your body language. Polite language use will be discussed later in the chapter.

CROSS REFERENCE

Participating in group seminars and meetings, Mind your language

- **Turn taking**. It is important to take turns in a way which ensures everybody is given the opportunity to speak, and no one person dominates the discussion. Turns can be long or short, ranging from leading the seminar, to putting forward a fairly detailed argument, to responding briefly to someone else's contribution. Those who facilitate seminars (lecturers and sometime students themselves) will often ensure that everyone gets a chance to speak, encouraging the quieter students to speak and more assertive ones to hold back a little.

- **Negotiating**. Negotiation is a part of the co-construction of meaning. It is part of the to-and-fro of dynamic discussion, of working out the facts and deciding what they mean. It involves asserting and questioning, confirming and clarifying, and agreeing and disagreeing. Negotiation is also a necessary part of organising and facilitating group interaction. This may involve deciding how to proceed at a particular part of the discussion – eg whether to move on to the next topic, summarise the discussion so far, or perhaps even take a vote.

CROSS REFERENCE

Participating in group seminars and meetings, Helping to construct meaning

- **Giving and eliciting confirmation and clarification**. As mentioned in the previous point, this forms part of the negotiation and co-construction of meaning. Confirming what you meant by something or asking someone else what they meant by something is an important part of discussion, as is providing or asking for clarification. These things help ensure that people do not reach conclusions based on a lack of information or on misunderstanding.

CROSS
REFERENCE

*Academic
Writing and
Referencing
for your
Education
Degree,*
Chapter 3,
Referring to
sources

- **Acknowledging others' ideas**. The importance of this is often underestimated in seminars. In academia, it is essential that contributions to a field are fully acknowledged. Similarly, in a seminar or other group discussion, it is important to acknowledge how what you say repeats or builds on what someone else has said, using phrases such as 'As Annie said...' or 'Just to add to what Paul was saying about parental involvement...'. This is important in a seminar for two reasons: 1) It reflects the value academia places on source attribution and avoidance of plagiarism; 2) It facilitates the flow of a discussion: if people repeat the same idea or a similar idea without signalling that it repeats or relates closely to what someone else has said, the discussion can become static and fragmented; acknowledging how ideas are connected and build on each other contributes to the smooth flow of the discussion.

- **Setting some ground rules**. If you do this at the beginning of the process – in your first seminar meeting with a particular group – it can help facilitate group interaction and avoid friction. The following **case study** relating the experiences of a university lecturer illustrates the point.

Case study

There are some students who always come late to seminars or don't do the preparatory work beforehand. This irritates other students who have, on many occasions, waited for the seminar to end so they can complain directly to me about this behaviour in the hope that I will confront these 'wayward' students. When I explain that the philosophy behind group work in seminars is such that students should challenge each other over unacceptable behaviour rather than depend on a lecturer to discipline and control, the students often say that they don't like challenging their peers, especially if they otherwise get on with them! I have given tips about how to broach the subject using such phrases as 'I'm sorry, this is nothing personal but we're supposed to be working as a group so it's important we all do what we're supposed to do'. Setting clear ground rules beforehand can help, as can reminding students that dealing with difficult situations (and people) is an inherent part of teaching practice so it is something they have to get used to.

Transferable skills

Seminar skills are important if you are to participate effectively in seminars – this goes without saying. However, it is also important to understand that many of the skills you develop in seminars are transferrable, ie useful in other areas of life, in particular, in your professional practice. These transferable skills include:

- meeting skills (eg interaction, turn taking, reaching a consensus, polite disagreement);
- intellectual skills (criticality, creativity);

- communication skills;
- linguistic skills;
- collaborative skills;
- social skills;
- intercultural skills.

These relate in particular to Part 2 of the Teachers' Standards (DfE, 2011), which require a teacher to demonstrate consistently high standards of personal and professional conduct.

Meetings in a professional setting

As a teacher, you will be required to attend, and indeed facilitate, many different types of meeting. These could be staff meetings, subject meetings, year group or phase meetings, disciplinary meetings (hopefully as a panel member and not as the person being disciplined!), case conferences and various types of committee. The skills required for these meetings are similar to those required for seminars, eg listening to the viewpoints of others and putting yours across assertively, being polite and diplomatic in your demeanour, sharing appropriate information and helping negotiate solutions to problems.

Mind your language

We all know that, in many situations, it's not what we say, but how we say it that counts. Notions of acceptable interaction can be different among different individuals and different cultures. Some individuals are more direct than others and may even come across as quite blunt; others are less direct and more circumspect in their interactions, and may even come across as lacking in assertiveness. Similarly, patterns of interaction which are acceptable in one culture may not be acceptable in another.

Case studies

A

While running a workshop on seminar skills, I was approached by a lecturer from overseas who was distraught by the fact that she seemed to be upsetting some students in her seminars. After some discussion, it became apparent that the lecturer would ask a question, and, if the answer was not what she was looking for, she would simply say 'no' and ask someone else. This had appeared to make some students uncomfortable, but she had no idea why, as this way of interacting had been perfectly acceptable in her home university. I explained that British people are generally more comfortable with less direct responses, particularly in a group situation where they might feel under scrutiny. We discussed the use of typical expressions we might use in this situation in order to 'soften' or 'cushion' what we say, such as 'I think I see what you mean but…', 'I take your point but…', 'I'm not quite sure that really addresses the point…'. The lecturer was surprised by this indirect approach as it did not match the conventions of her own culture, which allowed for a more direct approach, but she was nevertheless keen to try out the phrases in class as her main concern was that students should feel they were in a comfortable learning environment.

B

I was teaching a group of Mongolian students on an academic skills course. One of the main activities was a seminar. I was extremely impressed with the amount of preparation they had done and with the quality of their contributions. In particular, I noticed that they had all used really interesting examples from the media to support their arguments. I mentioned this later, while giving general feedback to the group. They nodded eagerly when I mentioned the quality of the examples, but I had noticed that they hadn't seemed very impressed at the time – in fact, they had not reacted at all to each other's examples. So I asked the students if they had considered commenting positively during the seminar, by saying, for instance, 'I think that's a really good example'. They all laughed a little and explained that this felt a bit strange: 'We just wouldn't do that.' However, they did agree to give it a go in the next seminar.

Task

Softening your language

1) Here are some phrases from earlier in the chapter. Find the words or phrases in each group that 'soften' the students' contributions.

A

'Wouldn't you say that poverty is a factor here?'

"Aren't we forgetting the impact of peer pressure?'

'But didn't that study have a really small sample size?'

B

'I take your point, but what about parental involvement?'

'I see what you mean, but why is that important?'

C

'Could I just add something to what Nerumalia said?'

'Sorry, could you just explain what you mean by "alternative strategies"?'

'I didn't quite catch what you said about the stats.'

'I'm afraid I don't quite follow your point.'

'I don't really think that what you're suggesting is realistic, given the current financial crisis in schools.'

2) Match each group (A, B, C) to the correct explanation (i, ii, iii).

i) Some 'little' words like 'just', 'quite' and 'really' are often used to soften or cushion a request, comment or criticism. In some of these cases, the use of 'sorry' or 'I'm afraid' further softens the intervention.

ii) The 'negative' question form can seem less direct or challenging than a direct question form. Question tags like 'isn't it?' can also have the same effect. Tone of voice and intonation are also factors here.

iii) Some 'yes, but...' structures, sometimes called 'pivot' structures, can cushion a disagreement, as they serve to acknowledge the validity of the other person's opinion before begging to differ.

Top tips

Softening your language: a summary

Negative questions (these usually have 'not' in them in their abbreviated form '...n't'):

- 'Wouldn't you say...?'

- 'Don't you think...?'

- 'Aren't we forgetting...?'

'Pivot' expressions (note key use of 'but'):

- 'I see what you mean but...'

- 'I think I understand where you're coming from but...'

- 'I take your point but...'

Little words ('just', 'quite', 'really'):

- 'Can I just say that...'
- 'Could you just explain what you mean by...'
- 'I don't quite follow.'
- 'That's not quite what I mean.'
- 'I don't really understand what you mean.'
- 'That's not really relevant.'

Summary

This chapter has explored the skills you need to participate effectively in group discussions, including seminars and meetings. It has discussed the role seminars play in your university studies, and introduced conventions and language which are important in a seminar setting. It has also looked at how the skills you develop in seminars can transfer to your professional life, eg the teamwork activities and meetings you might have to engage in as an educational professional.

References

Alexander, A, Argent, S and Spencer, J (2011) *EAP Essentials: A Teacher's Guide to Principles and Practice*. Reading: Garnet Publishing Ltd.

Department for Education (2011) Teachers' Standards [online]. Available at: www.gov.uk/government/uploads/system/uploads/attachment_data/fi le/665520/ Teachers__Standards.pdf (accessed 26 February 2019).

Chapter 5
Getting the most from individual tutorials

Learning outcomes

After reading this chapter you will:

- have a good understanding of the role of tutorials in your studies;

- be better aware of the 'etiquette' of tutorials;

- have explored strategies which can help you to make the most of tutorials.

This chapter will help you to understand the role tutorials play in your academic studies and become better aware of the 'etiquette' associated with them. It will also provide you with strategies that can help you to make the most of this valuable, but usually very limited, time with your lecturers and advisers.

What is a tutorial?

A tutorial is a meeting with an academic member of staff. The Quality Assurance Agency for Higher Education (QAA) defines it as: 'a meeting involving one-to-one or small group supervision, feedback or detailed discussion on a particular topic or project' (2011, p 6). This could be with a **lecturer** on a particular module, including the **module leader**, or it could with be your **personal tutor**, a member of academic staff assigned to provide you with guidance and support.

In most universities, a tutorial is normally a one-to-one meeting, in contrast with a lecture or a seminar, where larger groups of students are present. (Indeed, in lectures, sometimes hundreds of students may be present.) Occasionally, however, there may be more than one student present – maybe two or three. In fact, in some universities, a tutorial can be synonymous with a seminar, a small discussion group. However, the QAA (2011, p 15) distinguishes tutorials from seminars in terms of 'the stronger emphasis they place on the role of the tutor in giving direction and feedback'. This differentiation is important because it tells you what you should expect from a tutorial: not just advice and guidance but, specifically, **direction and feedback**.

Tutorials are usually face-to-face meetings, though occasionally they are conducted over the phone or through some virtual meeting software like Skype rather than in person. Telephone tutorials are often more convenient than virtual meetings, as the latter require a stable, fast internet connection. However, virtual meeting software with video function has the advantage of retaining the nuances of body language present in most face-to-face meetings.

CROSS REFERENCE

Chapter 4, Participating in group seminars and meetings

Tutorials may be scheduled as part of your timetable, with each student being given a particular time slot to meet with their lecturers or personal tutors. Many lecturers have **office hours** where they meet students, usually on a one-to-one basis. Depending on the institution, department or individual lecturer, you may need to email to book a tutorial, or there may be an open 'drop-in' session, where lecturers deal with queries on a first-come-first-served basis.

It is a good idea to find out about the conventions for tutorials at the beginning of your studies. Universities are adult learning environments which promote individual student responsibility, so you might have to initiate a request for a tutorial rather than wait for your lecturer or personal tutor to contact you. You should be able to find guidelines on tutorials in your course handbook or module guide, or on your Virtual Learning Environment (VLE) – usually Blackboard or Moodle. Most lecturers will be quite flexible about meeting you individually if you email them to arrange an appointment – just try to give plenty of notice and an indication of flexible availability, and be aware of particularly busy times of year for lecturers, such as periods of marking immediately after exams.

Why do you have tutorials at university?

Tutorials, particularly one-to-one tutorials, are a valuable opportunity for individual contact time with a member of academic staff. They are a chance to speak to a lecturer or personal tutor about a number of possible issues, including:

- your academic progress;
- concepts and skills important to your studies;
- learning how to make good study and research choices;
- learning how to think, study and research independently;
- the mark and feedback you've received in a particular assignment;
- pastoral issues, ie your individual development and welfare.

Tutorials with a module lecturer are usually concerned with academic issues; tutorials with a personal tutor may address both academic and personal issues.

Tutorials provide important individual support with your studies. As the QAA states (2011, p 6), an individual tutorial is probably the best chance you will have to gain personalised '**direction and feedback**', and these can have a significant effect on your academic attainment. Lecturer **direction** could relate to an area of your studies which you have found particularly difficult to understand, or a particular skill which you need to work on. Individual **feedback** from your lecturers is something which is essential to progress in all areas of academic life, including academic writing and speaking, and all areas of your education studies, including your reflective portfolio or the development of your teaching skills.

Having a tutorial is especially important if you have failed a particular piece of work since the direction and feedback in these circumstances is normally designed to be remedial, that is, to help you succeed on a further attempt. You might also arrange an academic writing tutorial in this case (discussed in the next section).

Academic writing tutorials

Most universities provide one-to-one **academic writing tutorials**, sometimes known as **academic writing consultations**. This is an opportunity to meet with an expert in English language and academic skills to discuss a piece of your writing – either something still in progress or something you've already received feedback on from an education lecturer.

In the case of a piece of work in progress, the tutor will be able to provide advice on how to improve it before submission. Note that these tutorials do not constitute a proofreading service. Some of the discussion will relate directly to the piece of work in question – how you might improve organisation, grammar, punctuation, style or word choice – but the main aim is to provide information and advice which you can apply more generally, helping you to develop into a better academic writer. This might involve thinking about how to plan and organise ideas in a coherent way, or how to link ideas together to form cohesive paragraphs. Proofreading is a more mechanical process, usually involving checking grammar and punctuation at the surface level of text at the very end of the writing process. This would simply not be the best use of the writing tutor's expertise.

In the case of a piece of work that has already been marked, the tutor will be able to help you understand the mark and the feedback you received. For example, a lecturer's comment to 'use a more academic style' may be more concretely explained as 'here you should have avoided the word "get" – better to use "obtain" instead', or 'personal pronouns are essential in a reflective essay, but a critical or theoretical essay tends to be more impersonal in tone, so it's best to avoid phrases like "I think we should" – try using phrases like "there is a strong argument for" when giving your opinion'.

The fact that a writing tutor is not an expert in your academic subject can be very beneficial for you, as they can tell you if your explanations of educational concepts and theories are largely understandable (excluding very technical detail) to a general audience, as they should be. In this sense, the tutor assumes the role of a 'critical friend'.

Students are usually restricted to one tutorial per semester, or even one per year, so make sure that you use the opportunity well. An academic writing tutorial is not a silver bullet. It will not solve all your writing problems or turn you into a better writer overnight. Developing as a writer is an incremental process based on a cycle of practice and feedback from a range of academic staff over time. But a writing tutorial can kick-start the process in many cases. In our experience, for many students, it can be a 'light-bulb' moment when they begin to understand where they were perhaps going wrong, and what simple steps they can take to make noticeable improvements. However, you need to be open to discussing your work critically if you are to benefit. If you are overly defensive about what you have written, it will be difficult to move forward. Remember, you are trying to write for a *reader* (the lecturer who marks your work or the writing tutor, both of whom have experience of reading hundreds of essays every year), and this is a rare but

CROSS REFERENCE

Academic Writing and Referencing for your Education Degree, Chapter 1, Academic writing: text, process and criticality; Chapter 2, Coherent texts and arguments

CROSS REFERENCE

Academic Writing and Referencing for your Education Degree, Chapter 5, Preparing your work for submission, Editing and proofreading your final text

CROSS REFERENCE

Academic Writing and Referencing for your Education Degree, Chapter 4, Language in use

invaluable opportunity to talk to that reader about their actual experience when reading your work.

Personal tutors

The role of a personal tutor varies across institutions, faculties and schools. However, all personal tutors in some way act as a gateway to the wider institution. They will point you in the direction of the wide variety of student support and development services that most universities provide, so they should be the first person you contact if you feel you need extra support or training. Examples of the types of support and development services UK universities provide include:

- in-sessional support in English language, mainly directed at international students, eg grammar workshops or pronunciation classes;
- in-sessional support in academic skills focusing on areas such as academic reading (eg reading journal articles), academic writing (eg writing essays), academic listening (eg note-taking in lectures) and academic speaking (eg giving academic presentations or participating in seminars); this support may be directed at international students, but it is increasingly open to all students;
- academic writing tutorials;
- disability support;
- financial, housing and social support;
- counselling.

Personal tutors are normally the first choice in providing you with references for future study or employment, although other lecturers may also be able to do this.

Tutorials in teaching

Since teaching is a practice-based discipline, discussions of classroom practice often feature in tutorials on education courses. These discussions can take many forms (as you will see in the following case studies) and include:

CROSS
REFERENCE

Critical
Thinking
for your
Education
Degree,
Chapter 2,
Reflective
practice

- discussions with a module lecturer as to how you might apply theory to your area of interest for an assignment;
- discussions with your personal tutor about difficulties you are having with a particular placement;
- discussions with either module lecturers or personal tutors about the role of reflection in enhancing your own teaching practice;
- practical discussions about the organisation of educational services in your local area.

Case studies

Look at the case studies below. What might the students do in each case? How might they benefit from speaking to a lecturer or personal tutor in a one-to-one tutorial?

A

Sandra has had feedback on an essay which has caused her some concern. She worked very hard on the essay, but even though the feedback indicated that most of the content was relevant, it also stated that she needed to improve her academic writing skills. However, it doesn't really go into much detail, and she's not really sure what she's doing wrong. She has seen that the university runs a number of courses on academic writing, but she thinks these may be aimed at international students who don't speak English as a first language and need help with grammar (Sandra was born and educated in Leeds).

B

Paul's grandmother is very sick and has not been given long to live. She is back in his home town in the Republic of Ireland, but he is not sure if he will be able to get back to see her. He has always been very close to her and is feeling extremely upset. He is not able to focus on his studies at all.

C

Laila's teaching practice supervisor has been in touch with Laila's personal tutor saying that Laila hasn't been turning up for her weekly school placement and that, on the occasions she has turned up, she is often late. Laila's personal tutor asks to see her.

D

Mark is concerned that a couple of popular students in his peer group have been posting material on social media that he feels is incompatible with the Teachers' Standards. However, he is worried that there might be repercussions if he reports them, eg that the rest of the group might ostracise him or call him a troublemaker, or that he might be jeopardising someone's future career by reporting them.

E

Shazia overheard a pupil refer to her using a racist term. She's upset about this, particularly as the pupil had always appeared pleasant to her. The pupil had not said anything offensive directly to her; she had just heard it while she was looking for materials in the class storeroom. She later mentioned this to her school mentor, who told her it was 'just part of the job' and she should 'toughen up'. This has made Shazia think about leaving teaching despite the fact that it has always been her dream job.

Discussion of case studies

A

Many students struggle with academic writing, so it is important not to be embarrassed or bury your head in the sand. Sandra may be right that the academic writing courses on offer are aimed at international students, but in fact, most universities have come to realise that *all* students can have issues with academic writing, regardless of their background, and these universities are increasingly making academic writing courses more widely available. It is also true that universities often provide classes to help international students with grammar, but academic writing courses usually deal with much wider issues, such as structuring an essay, developing a clear argument and making appropriate reference to sources. Furthermore, it is not just international students who can benefit from polishing their grammar and punctuation! If Sandra has a one-to-one tutorial with the lecturer who marked the essay, they will be able to be more specific about which aspects of her writing need attention, and they will probably reassure her that she is not the only student dealing with these issues. Both lecturers and personal tutors will be able to provide more information on in-sessional writing courses or individual academic writing tutorials that the university provides.

CROSS REFERENCE

Academic writing tutorials

B

In the first instance, Paul's personal tutor would most likely explore with Paul ways of facilitating his return to his home country to be with his grandmother at the end of her life. Most courses allow students to interrupt their studies when they have major personal crises and to restart them later, once the crisis has been resolved. While students are often reluctant to interrupt, in hindsight most feel it was the right decision. Sometimes, it is not possible for a student to interrupt their studies, perhaps because of financial reasons or because the course regulations have a limit on time allowed to complete a course. If it is not possible for Paul to interrupt his studies, his personal tutor would probably explore ways of supporting him while he remained at the university: this might even include referral to the counselling service. His personal tutor would probably also explore practical issues such as helping him obtain extensions on assignment deadlines or preparing a case for 'extenuating circumstances' in case he performed poorly in his assessments.

C

Laila's personal tutor will probably want to get to the root of the problem, as there are many reasons for students missing placements. Once the root of the problem has been established, her personal tutor can advise on a specific plan of action.

Sometimes, the root of the problem is students not understanding the professional obligations of teaching, such as good timekeeping and the importance of being courteous (eg by apologising if late), but, more often than not, it is down to personal issues such as disillusionment with the course or relationship problems. If it's about not understanding professional obligations, any feedback given to Laila is likely to be stern and straight to the point. It is important that Laila is in no doubt about the importance of professional standards in teaching. If it's about disillusionment, Laila's personal tutor might explain that most students get disillusioned at some point and they might further explore the situation to see if there are particular issues with this specific placement, such as poor supervision or intense workload. If it's about relationship problems, the student may well be signposted to other support services in the university, such as the counselling service.

D

Mark could raise this with a module lecturer or his personal tutor. They will most likely draw Mark's attention to Part 2 of the Teachers' Standards (DfE, 2011) which states that: 'A teacher is expected to demonstrate consistently high standards of personal and professional conduct'. But they will understand the predicament he finds himself in. They are likely to offer suggestions as to how he can fulfil his professional obligation to raise concerns while at the same time protecting himself from repercussions.

E

Shazia would benefit from discussing this with her personal tutor; it is a good case for a reflective discussion, not only in terms of how Shazia felt herself, but how she felt she was treated by the mentor. The personal tutor would most likely explore ways in which Shazia might address such issues in the future while still maintaining a passion for teaching. Her personal tutor might also sensitively explore with Shazia whether she wanted to challenge – perhaps even formally complain about – the mentor's comments.

Getting the most from tutorials

Be prepared

The lecturer's time is undoubtedly very limited, so spend time thinking about how you can make the best use of this valuable one-to-one, face-to-face meeting time. It is a good idea to prepare by making some notes or forming some focused questions.

CROSS
REFERENCE

Chapter 1,
Professional
speaking
skills,
Questioning
techniques

Ask the right questions

There are different types of question in English. See Chapter 1 for a detailed list and explanation of these. The type of question you use can have an impact on the interaction between you and the lecturer, and on how you are perceived. Understanding the difference between 'closed' and 'open' questions can be very helpful. These question types are discussed in detail in Chapter 1 of this book, but some examples relevant to tutorials are given below.

- **'Closed'** or **'yes/no'** questions usually only require a one-word, or at least short, answer, eg:

  'Would it be better to start my essay with some background and contextual information?'

  'Is withdrawal from the classroom to work with teaching assistants useful for children with English as an additional language?'

- **'Open'** or **'wh-'** questions usually elicit a more expansive answer, eg:

  'How should I start my essay?'

  'What strategies are useful for children with English as an additional language?'

Reflection

Both types of question outlined above have their place in any conversation, including the one you have with a lecturer in a tutorial. However, think about how the different types of question might affect the interaction in a tutorial and how they might affect the perceptions of the lecturer.

1)

'Would it be better to start my essay with some background and contextual information?'

versus

'How should I start my essay?'

2)

'Is withdrawal from the classroom to work with teaching assistants useful for children with English as an additional language?'

versus

'What strategies are useful for children with English as an additional language?'

Discussion of reflection

In this case, the closed questions may have some advantages (though this does depend on the particular context):

- They are usually easier and quicker to deal with, and tutorial time is usually quite limited.
- They can show the lecturer that you have already done some thinking yourself. The open questions in this case put the onus on the lecturer and ask them to do your thinking for you. The closed questions show that you have done some thinking yourself, and are now merely making good use of the expertise of the lecturer. It indicates that you are taking responsibility for your own learning, and that you are trying to learn independently. This will probably reflect positively on you and help facilitate a better relationship with the lecturer.

Check understanding

It can be difficult to take everything in when you are in a tutorial, so try to check understanding at certain points. You can do this by asking questions:

'Do you mean…?'
'Is that the same as…?'
'What was the name of the book you mentioned?'
'Could you just explain what you mean by…?'
'Can I just ask you about that last point…?'

You can also try to briefly summarise what you think is the main message and ask for confirmation:

'If I understand correctly, the term "SEND" includes…'
'Can I just check that I understand? Are you saying that…?'
'So, you're suggesting I compare these two approaches using the framework outlined in…?'

You can also state more directly that you haven't understood something by using the following polite phrases:

'I didn't quite catch what you said about…'
'I'm afraid I don't quite understand what you mean when you say that…'

Be assertive – but not rude!

Do not be afraid to be assertive. There might be points of disagreement between you and the tutor or lecturer, and this should be openly acknowledged. You just need to be careful that assertiveness doesn't tip over into rudeness. Negative questions can help 'soften' this type of exchange:

'Isn't it true that…?'
'Wouldn't it be better to…?'
'Don't you think that it would be better to…?'
'Doesn't that depend on…?'

CROSS REFERENCE

Chapter 4, Participating in group seminars and meetings, Mind your language

And the use of 'pivot' phrases to disagree can also be effective:

> 'I see what you mean, but…'
>
> 'I understand what you're saying, I just thought that…'

Notice the use of 'softening' words such as 'just', 'quite' and 'really'. This is discussed in more detail in Chapter 4 of this book.

Take notes

It is a good idea to take a few notes during a tutorial. Lecturers will be expecting you to do this. Later, you can review the notes to make sure you've understood everything. If there are action points to follow up on, or there's anything that doesn't seem to make sense, email as soon as possible ('Can I just confirm that…?' 'Could you please send the reference you mentioned…?') while the conversation is still fresh in both your minds.

Summary

This chapter has explained the different types of tutorial that can form part of your university studies. It has discussed the important role that individual tutorials play in your academic and personal development, particularly in terms of personalised direction and feedback. It has provided guidance to help you make the most of this valuable time with your lecturers at university, focusing on a number of useful interactional and linguistic strategies.

References

Department for Education (2011) Teachers' Standards [online]. Available at: www.gov.uk/government/uploads/system/uploads/attachment_data/file/665520/Teachers__Standards.pdf (accessed 26 February 2019).

QAA (Quality Assurance Agency for Higher Education) (2011) Explaining Contact Hours: Guidance for Institutions Providing Public Information about Higher Education in the UK [online]. Available at: http://dera.ioe.ac.uk/10451/7/contact_hours_Redacted.pdf (accessed 28 April 2019).

Chapter 6
Networking

Learning outcomes

After reading this chapter, you will:

- have developed a better understanding of the concept of networking;

- have developed an understanding of the role that networking can play in your academic and professional life;

- have developed strategies to help you network effectively in both face-to-face and virtual contexts;

- be better equipped to manage the opportunities and challenges presented by social media and other online platforms.

This chapter explores the role of networking in your education studies. Networking involves interacting with other people in order to exchange information and knowledge, or to develop social and professional contacts and associations. This chapter will explore the different networking platforms – whether face to face or virtual – available to students and teachers. It will allow you to reflect on your current networking skills, and on your current relationship with social media and other online platforms. It will explore what kind of networking-related activities and behaviours are appropriate for students and teachers. It will also help you to refine your networking skills so that you can use them to good effect in your academic and professional life.

Opportunities and challenges related to networking

There are a number of opportunities and challenges associated with networking. Networking activities can:

- provide **mutual academic and professional support**;
- facilitate the **sharing of information and knowledge**;
- present **opportunities for collaboration**;
- support **personal and professional development**.

Challenges associated with networking activities relate to:

- the need for a certain degree of **confidence** and well-developed **'soft skills'**, ie **communication skills** and **people skills**, also referred to as **interpersonal skills** (as opposed to subject-specific knowledge or pedagogic skills);

- widely reported **concerns surrounding social media and other online platforms**, mainly related to **security** and **reputation**.

These opportunities and challenges will be discussed in later sections of this chapter.

Different types of networking

There are many different ways to network as a student and as a teacher. **Conferences** are a longstanding, well-established forum for academics, students and professionals to come together to share research, experience, knowledge and ideas. Such gatherings provide an obvious opportunity for people to network both formally and informally. Professional organisations, such as the Chartered College of Teaching, also provide networking opportunities through local and national **meetings**, as well as conferences. Since the start of the twenty-first century, **social media** and other **online platforms** have also become increasingly important for networking.

Education students come to university with varying degrees of exposure to the different networking platforms, both for professional and for social purposes. The following task allows you to reflect on your current knowledge and experience of these platforms.

Task

1) Complete the table according to your experience of these types of networking, ie:

   a) how often you do these things;
   b) your purpose in using them;
   c) your likes and dislikes.

	a) HOW OFTEN			b) PURPOSE		c) LIKES/ DISLIKES		
	OFTEN	SOME-TIMES	NEVER	PERSONAL USE	USE FOR STUDY OR WORK	😊	😐	😞
Conferences								
Professional organisation meetings								
Traditional sports/social clubs or societies								

	a) HOW OFTEN			b) PURPOSE		c) LIKES/ DISLIKES		
	OFTEN	SOME-TIMES	NEVER	PERSONAL USE	USE FOR STUDY OR WORK	☺	😐	☹
Political/ activist groups								
Facebook								
LinkedIn								
Twitter								
Instagram								
YouTube								
Snapchat								
WhatsApp								
Chatrooms								
Discussion boards*								
Writing/ reading blogs**								
Teaching blogs or chatrooms								

* for example on a VLE such as Blackboard or Moodle
** online public diaries

2) Discuss and compare your table with other students. Discuss the reasons behind your usage and preferences.

3) Now you've heard about other people's experience and preferences, are there any forms of networking which you might think about doing, or doing more (or less!), or doing differently?

4) What factors do you consider when creating your **profile** for the social media sites that you use?

5) Look at the profile in the following case study. Do you think this is a good online profile for a student teacher? Give reasons.

Case study

Example online professional profile

Tony Smith

22 years old, student teacher (primary teaching), University of Anytown

I am an enthusiastic second-year student teacher. I'm also a keen scuba diver and avid sci-fi reader. I am heavily involved in supporting and fundraising for my local library and children's centre. I am committed to this as I believe it provides a platform for the local community to improve outcomes for young children and their families. It also helps reduce inequalities between families in greatest need and their peers in terms of child development and school readiness, as well as parenting aspirations and parenting skills.

As a student teacher, I am particularly interested in the role of early reading in developing school readiness and I am hoping to develop this area on qualifying as a primary teacher. I have some web design and coding skills that have sparked an interest in the potential of apps and other digital platforms in supporting development of reading for pleasure.

I am looking to network with other primary teachers and those interested in development of early reading/digital literacy for children and families.

Email: tony22@xyzmail.net

Education networking sites

Online education platforms/Twitter accounts allow teachers to find and share resources which are already available. In addition, collaborating with online colleagues can be an enlightening experience. This type of collaboration means that children have the opportunity to learn from all teachers and not just the ones teaching in their school. Blogs written by some experienced teachers can also be a source of continuing professional development for new teachers who may not have easy access to comparable sources.

Some particularly useful networking sites for teachers include:

- Chartered College of Teaching – https://chartered.college
- National Association for Special Educational Needs (NASEN) – www.nasen.org.uk
- National Association for the Teaching of English (NATE) – www.nate.org.uk
- National Education Union (NEU) – https://neu.org.uk
- The Association for Science Education (ASE) – www.ase.org.uk
- The Association of Teachers of Mathematics (ATM) – www.atm.org.uk

Some Twitter accounts that might be useful include:

- Association of Teachers of Mathematics (ATM) – @ATMMathematics
- Department for Education – @educationgovuk
- EAL (English as an Additional Language) Journal – @EAL_Journal
- E-Safety support.com – @ESafetySupport
- National Association for Language Development in the Curriculum (NALDIC) – @EAL_naldic
- National Association of Teachers of English (NATE) – @NATEfeed
- Schoolscience – @schoolscience
- The Association for Science Education (ASE) – @theASE
- Office for Standards in Education, Children's Services and Skills (Ofsted) – @Ofstednews
- UK Council for Internet Safety – @UK_SIC

Networking and the Teachers' Standards Part 2

All teachers and student teachers must make sure that their activities and behaviour are in line with the Teachers' Standards Part 2 (DfE, 2011).

Reflection

Look at the guidelines laid out by the Teachers' Standards Part 2 (DfE, 2011) below.

How do you think these broad principles could relate to the networking activities you discussed earlier in the chapter (face to face and virtual)?

A teacher is expected to demonstrate consistently high standards of personal and professional conduct. The following statements define the behaviour and attitudes which set the required standard for conduct throughout a teacher's career.

- Teachers uphold public trust in the profession and maintain high standards of ethics and behaviour, within and outside school, by:

  - treating pupils with dignity, building relationships rooted in mutualrespect, and at all times observing proper boundaries appropriate to a teacher's professional position

  - having regard for the need to safeguard pupils' well-being, in accordance with statutory provisions

  - showing tolerance of and respect for the rights of others

– not undermining fundamental British values, including democracy, the rule of law, individual liberty and mutual respect, and tolerance of those with different faiths and beliefs

– ensuring that personal beliefs are not expressed in ways whichexploit pupils' vulnerability or might lead them to break the law.

- Teachers must have proper and professional regard for the ethos, policies and practices of the school in which they teach, and maintain high standards in their own attendance and punctuality.

- Teachers must have an understanding of, and always act within, the statutory frameworks which set out their professional duties and responsibilities.

These principles are discussed in more detail in the rest of the chapter, particularly in relation to social media.

Conferences

Conferences are forums where academics, students and professionals gather to share research, experience, knowledge and ideas. There are usually a series of presentations where people present their research findings or describe some aspect of their work. There will usually be a **plenary** (a session attended by all participants of the conference) at the beginning and the end of the conference, usually led by a distinguished academic or professional in the field. People will then usually split into smaller groups for the other sessions. Formal academic **presentations** will often run alongside more informal **workshops** and **meetings**. All of these provide opportunities to meet and talk to people with similar academic and professional interests and concerns. For example, presentations usually end by opening up the floor with a question-and-answer session, and workshops provide important opportunities for group discussion. But it is often outside of these scheduled events that some of the most important networking occurs. Coffee and lunch breaks (and sometimes formal dinners or even excursions at longer conferences) are an excellent opportunity for people to catch up with acquaintances or former colleagues. They are also a chance to meet new people. Conferences are thus important networking platforms in addition to being important for the advancement of knowledge and the enhancement of professional practice.

The first conference you attend might feel a bit intimidating or even 'cliquey', but really what you're seeing is the effect of networking: these people who seem to know each other so well may also have been intimidated at their first conference, but they were brave enough to start a conversation that led to a professional relationship or even a personal friendship. There are a number of ways to be proactive: you might decide to speak to one of the presenters, or someone whose

ost-presentation question intrigued you; you might talk to someone from a
articular institution or organisation (information often included on name tags),
erhaps in relation to professional development.

Professional organisations

Many teaching and education-related professional organisations provide
opportunities for networking, whether face to face or online. Examples include
many subject organisations such as: the National Association for the Teaching of
English; the Association for Science Education (ASE); the Association of Teachers
of Mathematics (ATM). The National Education Union (NEU) is also important.
Most of the organisations mentioned above hold conferences every year. You
will probably need to pay a fee, ie a 'subscription', to become a member of these
organisations, but many offer cheaper rates for students. Most organisations
may have regional networking and professional development events that you
can attend, which can be useful for making new contacts and learning more
about what's happening in the field of education. National conferences and
regional special interest groups also offer excellent networking and research
opportunities. If you wish to contribute, while at the same time perhaps raising
your own profile in your field, you can volunteer to join committees and help
organise events.

The internet and social media

Most of you will probably have already developed a range of habits and skills
related to internet and social media use. These may include:

- communicating through social networking sites (eg Facebook, LinkedIn,
  Twitter);

- sharing online content, eg text, photos, video and audio files (eg on Twitter,
  Instagram, YouTube, WhatsApp, Snapchat);

- creating or using websites;

- writing or following blogs;

- contributing to discussion boards (eg on VLEs).

It is likely that you will be able to draw on this experience to develop your
professional networking skills. However, you may also have to reflect on your
internet and social media use, and possibly adapt your activity and behaviour
to suit your new academic and professional context. You are no doubt aware
of the current spate of debates surrounding the internet and social media. In
fact, there have been a number of recent media reports on teachers who have
been disciplined for inappropriate behaviour on social media, including lapses in
professionalism and breaches of confidentiality. Figures from the National College
of Training and Leadership disciplinary hearings show that 17 of the 100 hearings
held within a year stemmed from complaints about the use of social media sites,
with 16 of the 17 teachers being barred from the profession (Garner, 2014).

The following quote from an academic paper published in *Education and Information Technologies* (Fox and Bird, 2017) serves to remind how social media impacts on teachers today.

> Teachers, as other professionals, have lost their jobs as a result of their social media activity or been exposed to bullying, affecting them beyond the workplace into their personal lives with examples in Australia… the United States… and the United Kingdom… As well as responsibilities to themselves, teachers are additionally responsible for the pupils in their care.

Today, with the proliferation of social media platforms, any inappropriate talk could reach large numbers of people scattered far and wide, rather than just those people within earshot in public and professional spaces.

Social media and the Teachers' Standards

Social networking can be useful as a tool for collaborative planning, sharing resources, providing news and updates to pupils and parents, helping with homework and project assignments, promoting school and class achievement, recording and archiving lesson content for revision and keeping up to date with the latest pedagogy. A good example of this is the way in which a teacher in London can access a live feed of a conference in Toronto on Twitter as it happens, perhaps viewing PowerPoint slides or reading about audience reactions. Although the Teachers' Standards in the UK do not explicitly guide teacher behaviour on social media sites, they implicitly place responsibility on teachers to use social media in an effective and responsible manner. This is clear in Part 2, related to personal and professional conduct, as discussed earlier in the chapter. Other sections, for example 8, can also be related to social media use:

Fulfil wider professional responsibilities

- Make a positive contribution to the wider life and ethos of the school.
- Develop effective professional relationships with colleagues, knowing how and when to draw on advice and specialist support.
- Take responsibility for improving teaching through appropriate professional development, responding to advice and feedback from colleagues.
- Communicate effectively with parents with regard to pupils' achievements and well-being.

Using social media and the internet responsibly

Social media and the internet are useful, powerful tools which can inform us, entertain us and connect us. But they can also easily get out of control and lead to misunderstanding, embarrassment and even danger. This can cause problems in any aspect of your life. However, as a student and as a professional, the stakes are potentially very high. Irresponsible use of social media, including unlawful or unprofessional behaviour, can put your registration at risk. Behaviour of this type can include:

- sharing confidential information inappropriately;
- posting pictures of pupils or colleagues without their consent;
- posting inappropriate comments about pupils or colleagues;
- bullying, intimidating or exploiting pupils and colleagues;
- encouraging violence or self-harm;
- inciting hatred or discrimination;
- pursuing relationships with pupils or colleagues;
- stealing personal information or using someone else's identity.

Task

Make notes on how the actions and behaviours above contravene the Teachers' Standards Section 8, discussed above. They may contravene more than one Standard.

TEACHERS' STANDARDS PART 2	ACTION/ BEHAVIOUR CONTRAVENING STANDARD	NOTES
Make a positive contribution to the wider life and ethos of the school		
Develop effective professional relationships with colleagues, knowing how and when to draw on advice and specialist support		
Take responsibility for improving teaching through appropriate professional development, responding to advice and feedback from colleagues		
Communicate effectively with parents with regard to pupils' achievements and well-being		

Turkle (2011, p 259) in Fox and Bird (2017) states that if we accept the real and pervasive 'persistence of data' from social media use, teachers, as people with a particular status in society in terms of their responsibility to young people and their parents/carers, need to be upskilled and supported in how to capitalise on rather than be negatively affected by their digital footprints. It is also important to understand that pupils are also users of social media, and they may in fact attempt to contact their teachers through social media. The perceived informality of this medium can make it difficult to maintain professional boundaries. In fact, professional networking on social media does not normally include adding pupils you have taught to your social media accounts, even if they request it.

First and foremost, it is essential that your use of social media adheres to the regulations and guidelines issued by universities and employers, as well as by professional bodies. There are also general 'rules' of behaviour which can help you use social media and the internet in a responsible way.

Netiquette

It is not possible to cover every instance of social media use that you will encounter, but there are 'rules of thumb' that you can follow to help you to navigate this complex world safely, professionally and effectively. These rules are sometimes referred to as **'netiquette'** (a portmanteau of 'internet' and 'etiquette' – good manners in social interaction). The rules of netiquette can help to promote the professional behaviour expected of students and teachers. They can help protect you and others from harm and embarrassment. The following **top tips** box lists some netiquette rules which can guide you towards posting responsibly on social media.

Top tips

Posting responsibly

- **Be social media savvy.** Be aware of how the medium you are posting on works, and how to control any filters or privacy settings. Be clear about what other people will see or hear when you post. Take any action you can to protect yourself and others.

- **Think before you post.** You may come to regret an unguarded comment or an embarrassing photo. These could be seen by a prospective employer, for example. Also, avoid using social media to let off steam or complain about work or colleagues.

- **Post with integrity.** Post when you are in the right frame of mind and with the right intentions. Don't post after a night out, or when you are upset, for example. Also, avoid plagiarism, just as you would in an academic essay or presentation. Credit photos and cite authors. Don't pass off anything as your own if it isn't.

- **Post appropriately.** The use of social media spans our professional and personal lives, and this can sometimes lead us to blur the boundaries between them. While teachers can find social media a valuable forum for discussion, it is important to understand the constraints of such conversations. Your default tone should be one of politeness and restraint – though, of course, there are times when it is fine to be excited or effusive – when you are congratulating someone on an achievement for example. Also, remember, the Teachers' Standards (DfE, 2011) require you to 'demonstrate an understanding of and take responsibility for promoting high standards of literacy, articulacy and the correct use of standard English'. This means paying attention to grammar and punctuation. You should also avoid 'text language' when posting professionally. Also be aware that deleting a post does not necessarily mean it has not left a footprint.

- **Post professionally.** If in doubt, consider the Teachers' Standards Part 2. Ask your self if your post lives up to standards of personal and professional conduct.

Summary

This chapter has outlined the concept of networking and explored some of the different networking platforms available to students and teachers. It has looked at some of the behaviours and activities associated with networking, both face to face and online, and discussed what is considered to be appropriate for students and teachers, with particular reference to Teachers' Standards Part 2 (DfE, 2011). It has suggested ways in which you, as a student teacher, can refine your networking skills so that you can use them to good effect in your academic and professional life, as well as your personal life.

References

Department for Education (2011) Teachers' Standards [online]. Available at: www.gov.uk/government/uploads/system/uploads/attachment_data/file/665520/Teachers__Standards.pdf (accessed 23 March 2019).

Department for Education (2018) *Keeping Children Safe in Education* [online]. Available at: https://assets.publishing.service.gov.uk/government/uploads/system/uploads/attachment_data/file/741314/Keeping_Children_Safe_in_Education__3_September_2018_14.09.18.pdf (accessed 18 April 2019).

e-safetysupport.com (2014) *What Every Teacher Needs to Know About Social Media* [online]. Available at: www.staidanscatholicacademy.co.uk/wp-content/uploads/2015/02/What-every-teacher-needs-to-know-about-social-media.pdf (accessed 23 March 2019).

Fox, A and Bird, T (2017) The Challenge to Professionals of Using Social Media: Teachers in England Negotiating Personal-Professional Identities. *Education and Information Technologies*, 22(2): 647–75 [online]. Available at: https://link.springer.com/article/10.1007/s10639-015-9442-0 (accessed 23 March 2019).

Garner, R (2014) Twice as Many Teachers Banned This Year for Misusing Social Media. *The Independent* [online]. Available at: www.independent.co.uk/news/education/education-news/twice-as-many-teachers-banned-this-year-for-misusing-social-media-9880229.html (accessed 23 March 2019).

Turkle, S (2011) *Alone Together: Why We Expect More from Technology and Less from Each Other*. New York: Basic Books.

Appendix 1
Academic levels at university

UNDERGRADUATE STUDY			
England, Wales, Northern Ireland	**Scotland**	**Award**	**Notes**
Level 4	Level 7	Certificate of Higher Education (CertHE)	
Level 5	Level 8	Diploma of Higher Education (DipHE) Foundation Degree (FdD)	
Level 6	Level 9	Ordinary Bachelor Degree eg BA Education	Minimum academic qualification for teachers in England, Wales and Northern Ireland
	Level 10	Bachelor Degree with Honours eg BA (Hons) Education, BEd (Hons)	Usual academic qualification for teachers in England, Wales and Northern Ireland
POSTGRADUATE STUDY			
Level 7	Level 11	Masters Degree, eg MSc, MA, MPhil Postgraduate Certificate or Diploma (PGCert; PGDip)	Useful qualification for those wishing to advance their career
Level 8	Level 12	Research Doctorate (PhD) Professional Doctorate	Useful qualification for advancing careers, especially for working in teacher education in universities

Appendix 2
Key phrases in assignments

analyse	Mostly levels 5 and 6, especially with the word 'critically'; rarely level 4	Look at the concepts and ideas under discussion in depth; the addition of 'critically' means look at the concepts and ideas in depth **and** with a critical eye
assess	All levels, though common at lower levels	Make comments about the value/ importance of the concepts and ideas under discussion
compare	All levels, though common at lower levels	Look for similarities between the concepts and ideas under discussion
contrast	All levels, though common at lower levels	Look for differences between the concepts and ideas under discussion; often used with 'compare' (see above)
define	All levels, though common at lower levels	State precisely what is meant by a particular issue, theory or concept
discuss	Level 5 and above; sometimes level 4	Give reasons for and against; investigate and examine by argument
evaluate	Mostly levels 5 and 6, especially with the word 'critically'	Weigh up the arguments surrounding an issue, using your own opinions and, more importantly, reference to the work of others
illustrate	All levels	Make clear by the use of examples
outline	All levels, though tends to be used with the lower levels	Give the main features of
review	All levels, though 'critically review' would imply level 5 and above	Extract relevant information from a document or set of documents
state	All levels, though tends to be used with the lower levels	Present in a clear, concise form
summarise	All levels, though tends to be used with the lower levels	Give an account of all the main points of the concepts and ideas under discussion
with reference to	All levels	Use a specific context, issue or concept to make the meaning clear

Appendix 3
English language references

This is not meant to be an exhaustive list of resources, but rather a selection of those that we have found most useful in our work with students.

Dictionaries

There are many online dictionaries, but if you prefer to feel the weight of one in your hands, then Chambers is a good choice:

Chambers 21st Century Dictionary (1999) Edinburgh: Chambers Harrap Publishers Ltd.

A good online dictionary, especially for students whose first language is not English, is the Cambridge Dictionary. The definitions are very clear and easy to understand, and there is an excellent pronunciation tool for students whose first language is not English:

Cambridge Dictionary [online]. Available at: http://dictionary.cambridge.org (accessed 28 April 2019).

Grammar books

Caplan, N (2012) *Grammar Choices for Graduate and Professional Writers*. Ann Arbor, MI: University of Michigan Press.

Caplan's book is aimed at postgraduate students (known as 'graduate' students in the USA, where this book is published). Nevertheless, if you are looking for a systematic analysis of English grammar in the context of academic English, you may find this book very useful. It contains many clear examples of grammar in use in real-life academic writing.

Hewings, M (2015) *Advanced Grammar in Use*. 3rd ed. Cambridge: Cambridge University Press.

Murphy, R (2015) *English Grammar in Use*. 4th ed. Cambridge: Cambridge University Press.

Murphy, R (2015) *Essential Grammar in Use*. 4th ed. Cambridge: Cambridge University Press.

The Grammar in Use series is particularly useful for students whose first language is not English. The books present each grammar point in a clear and systematic way, and provide exercises and a self-study answer key. There are also lots of multimedia features in recent editions.

Other resources

Academic Phrasebank [online]. Available at: www.phrasebank.manchester.ac.uk (accessed 28 April 2019).

Academic Word List [online]. Available at: www.victoria.ac.nz/lals/resources/academicwordlist (accessed 28 April 2019).

Baily, S (2011) *Academic Writing for International Students of English.* 3rd ed. Oxon: Routledge.

Bottomley, J (2014) *Academic Writing for International Students of Science.* Oxon: Routledge.

Peck, J and Cole, M (2012) *Write it Right: The Secrets of Effective Writing.* 2nd ed. New York: Palgrave Macmillan.

Swales, J and Feak, C (2012) *Academic Writing for Graduate Students: Essential Tasks and Skills.* 3rd ed. Michigan: Michigan ELT.

Answer key

Chapter 1, Professional speaking skills

Being a good communicator

Task: Active listening (page 13)

1) Acknowledging what the pupil has said; restating and reflecting back to the pupil what they have told you to check that you understand correctly.

2) First part of the response demonstrates active listening – echoing, clarification; second part explores the issue in an attempt to be empathic.

3) Example of active listening by both the teacher and the parent, which is typical in flowing conversations; involves restating and clarifying.

4) Active listening allows teachers/tutors to pick up on the pupil's desire to find a solution; acknowledges that the pupil wants to change and starts exploring this issue further.

Chapter 2, Professional writing skills

Record keeping

Task: Avoiding jargon (page 30)

Faisal displays elements of dyslexia and finds learning many basic grapheme–phoneme correspondences (GPCs) in systematic synthetic phonics lessons challenging. There are indications of Attention Deficit Hyperactivity Disorder (ADHD). Suggest home school liaison officer makes contact with parents as soon as possible.

Writing reports

Task (pages 33–34)

1) A Executive summary

   B Introduction

   C Recommendations

2) A a) carried out; b) solve knife crime; c) help and prevention

   B a) protect; b) searching for answers; c) and sometimes conflicting

   C a) involve; b) strategies; c) knife

Writing reports
Task (page 35)

Recommendation

Phonics has become a key consideration in the teaching of reading, and greater emphasis is now placed on phonic approaches and their effectiveness in teaching children to read. There will be a review of the phonics approaches in this scheme, in order to bring the texts in line with current research.

Writing official letters
Task (pages 36–38)

1) Which address is that of a) the sender and b) the recipient?

The sender's is in the top right-hand corner; the recipient's is on the left, slightly lower down the page.

2) What does 're' (first line of the letter) mean?

'Regarding'. This is a common way of starting an official letter as it makes the topic immediately clear; in this case, the parent's name is given prominence.

3) The letter starts with 'Dear Mrs Parent' and ends with 'Yours sincerely'. When would you end a letter with 'Yours faithfully'?

See the **Top tips** box immediately following the letter.

4) What is the purpose of the letter?

The purpose is to inform parents about their child's conduct and the reason sanctions have been taken against him.

5) Who will read the letter?

The letter will be read by Mrs Parent. Mrs Boss is copied in (cc) at the end of the letter, which means she will receive an exact copy (cc is short for 'carbon copy') of the letter.

6) Is the language used in the letter suitable for all readers?

The language is formal but accessible. The letter has a conversational, narrative style which makes it easy to relate to and follow (most of us are used to story-telling in books and on TV). Mrs Parent, as well as the headteacher, will be able to understand easily.

7) Does the letter conform to the guidelines described in previous sections of this chapter?

The letter mostly avoids jargon and uses 'plain English'. There are no esoteric educational terms and most of the words used are part of most people's vocabulary.

The letter is scrupulously transparent – events are clearly specified; statements are carefully backed up with reference to evidence from other people. Although the letter addresses a serious behaviour issue, it ends on a positive note and invites Mrs Parent to contact the school if she wishes to discuss the matter further.

Chapter 3, Academic presentations and public speaking

Giving effective academic presentations

Task: Organising information and ideas (page 47)

All should start with an introduction:

- Introduction
  - about myself;
  - aims/structure of the session;
  - any ground rules (eg ask questions at end or it's fine to interrupt).

They should end with:

- wrap up/summary and any questions;
- a 'take-home message' if possible.

Possible structures:

1) **The teaching family in schools in the twenty-first century.**

   - The teaching family
     - Explore workers loosely categorised as 'teachers':
       - Teaching assistants (TAs)
       - Higher level teaching assistants (HLTAs)

- o Student teachers
- o Supply teachers
- o Peripatetic teachers
- o Unqualified teachers
- o Qualified teachers
- Outline debate over what a teacher is, focusing on qualified teachers and claims of attempts to 'dumb down' the profession
  - Argument that qualified teachers should be graduates
- Workforce and skill mix
  - Necessity of skill mix
  - Skill mix and pupil development
- The future teacher
  - Changing face of schooling
  - What future education system might look like and requirements of the teaching family

2) **The role of teaching assistants and higher level teaching assistants.**
- What are teaching assistants?
  - Definitions
  - Facts and figures
- What roles do they perform?
  - Can they replace teachers?
  - Do they have unique skills?
  - Is there a limit to their potential involvement in teaching?
- Examples of ways in which teaching assistants are deployed

3) **Supporting children with learning difficulties.**
- What are learning difficulties?
  - Facts and figures
  - Examples of support strategies
- Are there limits to what class teachers can do?
  - When is specialist support needed?
- The role of different types of teacher in supporting children with learning difficulties

Chapter 4, Participating in group seminars and meetings

The role of seminars in universities

Task (pages 64–65)

4)

a) Seminars provide an opportunity to follow up on a lecture. They allow you to demonstrate your understanding of the topic, and to clarify anything that you didn't understand from the lecture itself. **both**

b) Seminar discussion can enable you to forge a deeper understanding of ideas and concepts. **thinking**

c) Seminar discussions can be good preparation for essays, exams and other assessments, as they provide a space for you to test your understanding and ideas, and work out how to express them in a clear, convincing way. **both**

d) Seminars provide an opportunity to learn from people with different knowledge, background, experience and perspectives from your own. **thinking**

e) Seminar discussion may lead you to change, develop or adapt your opinions and ideas as you come into contact with others' views. **thinking**

f) Some seminar activities can help you develop your problem-solving skills. **thinking**

g) Frequent participation in seminars can help you become more confident about public speaking. **communication**

h) Seminars can help you become more confident about discussing complex issues and ideas. **communication**

i) Seminars can help you improve the way you interact with others in a group setting. **communication**

j) Seminar skills are transferable skills which can help you in your professional practice, for example in teamwork and meetings with colleagues. **communication**

The conventions of seminars

Task (pages 68–69)

1) 'Wouldn't you say that poverty is a factor here?' **politely/cautiously/challenging/contributing**

2) 'Yes, but what about parity of opportunity between the private and maintained sectors?' **politely/challenging/contributing**

3) 'But surely that's the role of government?' **politely/challenging/disagreeing**

4) 'What do you think, Harriet?' **politely/cautiously/challenging/contributing**

5) 'As Faisal said, the policy seems to disadvantage children from poorer homes and advantage the government, who essentially save money by putting the onus on parents.' **acknowledging contributions/reformulating**

6) 'I think Finland is a good example of somewhere where state education is given a high priority.' **making a contribution to the discussion**

7) 'Did you say you worked with children with dyslexia on your placement, Lia?' **inviting participation**

8) 'Could I just add something to what Nerumalia said?' **acknowledging contributions and building on them**

9) 'Aren't we forgetting the impact of peer pressure?' **politely challenging/ contributing**

10) 'But isn't that more an issue of compliance? Or is it "concordance" or "adherence" that we use now?' **politely/cautiously/challenging/contributing/ clarifying/checking**

11) 'I take your point, but what about parental involvement?' **politely challenging**

12) 'I see what you mean, but why is that important?' **politely challenging/ disagreeing**

13) 'According to one of the studies we were asked to look at, there is some evidence to suggest that the strategy can be effective if it is combined with other strategies.' **supporting ideas with evidence**

14) 'But didn't that study have a really small sample size?' **challenging**

15) 'I didn't quite catch what you said about the stats.' **asking for clarification**

16) 'Sorry, could you just explain what you mean by "alternative strategies"? I ask because lots of different strategies with widely varying evidence bases get lumped together under that heading.' **asking for clarification**

17) 'I'm afraid I don't quite follow your point.' **asking for clarification**

18) 'So what you're saying is that we need to provide different types of support.' **reformulating/checking**

19) 'Yes, that's a really good example.' **acknowledging contributions**

20) 'Yes, I hadn't thought of that.' **acknowledging contributions**

21) 'Are you sure about that? It's not how I interpreted it.' **politely/cautiously disagreeing**

22) 'I don't really think that what you're suggesting is realistic, given the current financial crisis in schools.' **politely disagreeing**

23) 'Are we all agreed on that?' **reaching consensus**

Mind your language

Task (pages 74–75)

2)

   A (ii)
   B (iii)
   C (i)

Index

Note: **bold** page numbers refer to tables.